START & RUN A MEDICAL PRACTICE

DR. MICHAEL CLIFFORD FABIAN

Self-Counsel Press
(a division of)
International Self-Counsel Press Ltd.
USA   Canada

Self-Counsel Press acknowledges the financial support of the Government of Canada through the Book Publishing Industry Development Program (BPIDP) for our publishing activities.

Printed in Canada.

First edition: 2010

Library and Archives Canada Cataloguing in Publication

Fabian, Michael Clifford
        Start & run a medical practice / Michael Clifford Fabian.

ISBN 978-1-55180-892-5

        1. Medicine — Practice — Canada. 2. Medical offices — Canada — Management.
I. Title. II. Title: Start and run a medical practice.
R728.F32 2010   610.68′1   C2010-900477-9

Cover Image
Copyright©iStockphoto/Charts & Stethoscope/Hogie

Inside Image
Copyright@iStockphoto/Heartbeat/Rinelle

Mixed Sources
Cert no. SW-COC-001271
© 1996 FSC

FSC

Self-Counsel Press
(a division of)
International Self-Counsel Press Ltd.

1704 North State Street	1481 Charlotte Road
Bellingham, WA 98225	North Vancouver, BC V7J 1H1
USA	Canada

CONTENTS

3. IMPORTANT INFORMATION TO KNOW BEFORE YOU BEGIN

4. CHOOSING THE TYPE OF OFFICE PRACTICE

CHECKLISTS

SAMPLES

NOTICE TO READERS

PREFACE

To start and run a health-care practice is a continuum — from the time you think about a career in a medical field to the day you finally take down the shingle, and everything in between. None of the steps along the way can be considered in isolation as each and every part of the journey plays a key role as to how your career, or practice, will shape up in the end.

Having a fulfilling career in a medical field, or in any career for that matter, is based on having sound motivation, goals, and expectations for what lies ahead. Also, doing due diligence when it comes to researching the field before you dive into things head first will make for a happy camper in the long run! The office staff who are involved in a medical practice will also understand and appreciate things so much better if the appropriate background is gained at the outset.

While much of this book is focused on practicing as a medical doctor, there is significant overlap between the different health-care professions. Much of what is covered in this book can be applicable to any of the allied health-care professions and thus will be of interest to people in similar careers. Many medical offices are multidisciplinary in the first place, with medical doctors working alongside colleagues in other health-related fields. It is for this reason that a wide audience can relate to setting up a career and practice in a health-care related field.

While I have mostly learned though personal experience as to how to start and run a medical practice, I often wished I had a resource like this book to help me with the choices and the challenges I had in the beginning. Also having realistic ideas of what lies ahead before making those life-changing decisions is paramount. No matter what stage of the journey you are at, what decisions you have ahead, which health-care field you are in, or what your intent is in reading this book, I hope that you will find the content helpful and relevant to your needs.

INTRODUCTION

Starting up a new medical practice is a very exciting time in a person's life. There are, however, so many considerations, decisions, and challenges along the way, that the experience can be quite daunting.

Some readers will be looking for a more holistic evaluation of what it's like to be in a medical or allied health profession before deciding on this career route. For those of you who are already in the career, it is not a bad idea to reflect on the reasons as to why you chose a medical career in the first place, before getting into the fine details of how you can set up an office. On the one hand, you may need to go back to the basics of your reasoning for pursuing a medical career, and keep reminding yourself of your good intentions. On the other hand, while you might be choosing this career path for all the right reasons, you have no idea what your future actually entails until you finish your training and have started working.

I have come across people, myself included, who are already way down the career path and realize that there are parts of the profession they had no idea about. The more you find out about things before you jump in at full throttle, the better off you will be.

Medical-related offices are so much alike no matter what health-care field you are in, or planning to be in. I have included many of the allied health fields at some point in the book, as there is so much similarity in practice dynamics and patterns. It is for this reason that I feel this book will benefit anyone who is interested in setting up an office in any health-care field. (See Chapter 1 for more information about the allied health fields.)

Some of the information in this book might also be relevant for any staff associated with running the office — having an understanding of the background and basic principles can only benefit the staff and the situation. I have tried not to always use the word "doctor" throughout the book because most of what is said relates to any health-care provider, so you shouldn't be dissuaded by terminology.

When you complete your training, or even if you have finished already, being informed beforehand is key to running a successful practice. On the one hand, hopefully, you will be in a supportive environment in which your colleagues located in the same area as your new practice will be there as valuable resources when it comes to any questions, or advice. On the other hand, there are hostile environments in which similar, or competing, professionals do not want a new person in the area. There are many reasons for this — competition and skill set being a couple examples of reasons why someone might want to keep new people out of the "territory" — in which an additional health-care provider can be seen as a threat to their practice and livelihood. I have been in both these situations, and in the latter you can feel quite alone, and certainly unwanted, when trying to get things going. These are some of the reasons that I hope this book will be of value to you as a helpful resource guide.

As you read through the different chapters, you will come across a diverse overview of what it's like to get started. Most of this information is derived from personal experience, including observation, as well as active involvement in many start-ups and already-running practice scenarios; I have also relied on the wisdom of others who have provided advice and insight into many of the topics covered. I have used alternate identification throughout the book so that no personal information is divulged in a way that it can be linked to an individual. I have also modified some stories ever so slightly when I feel the description, or circumstances, can potentially allow for some connection by the readers.

While I hope you will find the entire book interesting and appropriate for your own needs, some of the chapters might be of less interest to you personally. This book is designed in such a way that skipping a portion will not mean you have missed some "plot" and you will thus be lost for the remainder of the book! Each chapter has its own theme, and you will not be disadvantaged if you miss chapters or read the book out of sequence. Use it in your own way, as the intention of this book is to be of benefit to a broad audience — it's for anyone who is about to set up a medical-type office, is planning to set up an office in the future, or is currently involved in the functions of a medical office.

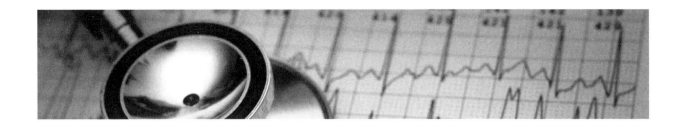

1

CAREERS SUITED TO OWNING AND OPERATING A MEDICAL-TYPE PRACTICE

The term medicine is used very broadly. In some ways it is a misnomer because much of what is done in the medical field is not related to medicine; most people equate medicine to some type of compound or solution. The practice of medicine encompasses so many different things other than just giving or taking medicine. In section **2.**, you will learn more about the many careers within medicine, or similar to medicine, that have nothing to do with "prescribed" medicine.

Having this background about the term "medicine" during the course of this book will allow you to appreciate the overlap with the allied health professions and medical doctors. Terminology does not always do justice — what's more important are the concepts and boundaries, particularly relating to starting a medical practice.

1. MEDICAL DOCTORS

A career as a medical doctor, often also referred to as a career in medicine, involves a training period that culminates in a professional qualification, and designation, and subsequent practice as a medical doctor. Even though a person becomes a medical doctor, it might end up that he or she actually has nothing to do with medicine.

The length of time and type of training can be dependent on the background of the individual, the institution, and the geographic location. It also depends on whether you factor in the education undertaken in order to get to the point of starting medical school, and all the training that occurs after the medical degree is completed.

The term "physician" does not always mean the same thing as "medical doctor." In some countries, particularly the United Kingdom (UK), a physician is a medical doctor who has done further training to become a specialist in general conditions relating to the adult (very similar to a pediatrician who is a specialist for children). The North American equivalent of the UK physician would be an internist, or a specialist in internal medicine. For the purpose of this book, I will be using the terms "medical doctor," "doctor," and "physician" interchangeably; all these terms referring to the same person.

One really confusing term also common in the UK, Ireland, and that region of the world is the designation "Mr.," which is used for doctors who have completed their surgical training and are now a consultant surgeon. They revert back to the "Mr." from "Dr." The equivalent would obviously apply for females as well.

The term physician is not only limited to a medical doctor. Certainly in North America, other health-care providers who utilize the nomenclature "physician" include podiatrists (i.e., foot specialist who has not gone through traditional medical school), osteopaths (i.e., a different training route to conventional medical school) and naturopathic physicians.

2. ALLIED HEALTH PROFESSIONS

Including a description of careers similar to medicine in this book is essential for several reasons. Firstly, for those individuals still deciding on what exactly to do in the health-care field, this will give an overview of the professions that are close in many ways to being a medical doctor. In addition to a description of what these professionals actually do, in some cases I have also provided more practical information, particularly relating to the collaborative nature of the allied health professions.

I have interacted with other health-care professionals who are similar to medical doctors in many different ways, and in a variety of clinical situations. The following examples will be both from my professional experiences, as well as personal encounters, with these individuals whose careers overlap significantly with medicine.

While many people initially pursue a career in medicine, there are many obstacles along the way, particularly relating to the application process and the associated competitive nature. I am a firm believer in that things happen for a reason, and if a person doesn't become a medical doctor, it wasn't meant to be! The limited number of seats for the vast number of applications is not restricted to medicine. Gaining acceptance into professional programs is just as hard — sometimes harder — for some of the careers that follow.

In terms of setting up a practice, I feel all the mentioned professionals could benefit from much of what is covered in this book — offices often function in a very similar fashion. The array of allied health fields with their own specialized and unique training are expanding rapidly, and I will not be able cover everything, and everyone, in the confines of this book, but I will certainly include the most common professions.

As you read through the different fields in the following sections, please keep in mind that I am primarily covering the professions similar to medicine in terms of an office setup. There are many domains that are closely affiliated with medicine, but they usually do not practice in the office setting. Some examples are paramedics, surgical assistants, and pharmacists — for this reason we will not discuss them in the following sections.

There are so many opportunities in exciting professions that are similar to medicine in many ways, including the practice and office setup. Some of them may have dimensions that you were not aware of, but the following sections are just a brief outline of the multitude of allied heath professions. It is for this reason that I feel parts of this book will benefit health-care providers other than just medical doctors, who plan to set up an office, wish to find out more about setting up a practice, or are just considering a career in a health-care related field.

In the Resources file on the CD you will find further information about the following careers.

2.1 Audiology

An audiologist primarily assesses hearing and the things associated with hearing. Audiologists are experienced with a battery of basic and advanced testing relating to the ear and hearing. They are experienced with hearing-aid devices and prescribe them when needed after the necessary investigations, sometimes in collaboration with physicians. Their practices can branch out into the occupational work environment, hospitals, academic domain, or even into involvement with the music and entertainment industry. They might work independently, in an academic setting, or in a health-care facility.

Audiologists work closely with physicians in many situations. The office setup is often identical to a doctor's office in terms of functionality. I have shared offices with audiologists, had them work in my office, as well as had a close working relationship with them in their independent offices.

2.2 Chiropractic

While in otolaryngology practice, I referred patients to chiropractors when the need arose.

While the practice of otolaryngology might assess conditions related to thyroid, salivary glands, voice box (larynx), neck glands, and tumors, problems related to the spine and muscles are something that otolaryngologists don't commonly take care of. With patient problems associated with the spine and muscles, depending on the situation for the patient, I would refer them to a chiropractor for assessment and treatment. Other options for referral of these patients were to orthopedic surgeons or physiotherapists — all depending on what the actual problem was.

Chiropractors go through rigorous training just like medical doctors, and there is much overlap in terms of assessment and treatment, particularly with physicians who deal with muscular skeletal problems (e.g., orthopedic surgeons, rehabilitation medicine specialists, and family physicians). Chiropractors do not generally work in hospitals, prescribe medicine, or do surgery. They may, however, perform acupuncture; something medical doctors do less often themselves.

Chiropractors' offices can look, and function, the same as any of their medical colleagues, or they can share facilities with other health professionals.

2.3 Dentistry

The dentistry field is very similar to medicine in so many ways, although the equipment needed to set up a dental office is vastly more complex and expensive than the average medical office. There are, however, some exceptions in the medical field in which cost can be comparable to a dentist's office; ophthalmology and cosmetic surgery being two such examples. I have a dentist friend who has always been envious of the minimum start-up cost of an average medical doctor's practice compared to that of a dentist!

I am aware of several individuals who have struggled between choosing a career in medicine versus dentistry. The medical school and dental school curriculum are so much alike, especially during the earlier years of training. Many universities across the globe combine the initial stages of the training of medical and dental students and integrate their initial basic science training. In fact, some schools have a combined college of medicine and dentistry with a single integrated administration.

I think everyone who is reading this book is very familiar with what dentists do, or at least I hope so! However, I am not sure if everyone is aware of the scope of their practice and know that dentists can specialize in many areas, where there is little differentiation in the way they practice compared to their medical colleagues. Oro-maxillo-facial surgery (otherwise known as oral surgery) is one such example. Dental surgeons typically do an additional four years of training after dental school and spend much of their time gaining exposure to medicine alongside their medical trainee colleagues. They operate, admit their patients, do surgery, and take care of them just like medical surgeons. The procedures they do are complex and can include cosmetic or reconstructive surgery of the head and neck. It is not uncommon for these highly trained surgeons to be dually qualified as both dentists and physicians, including their extra training in oral surgery.

There are times in which I have closely interacted with dentists as an otolaryngologist. Patients who have snoring and sleep apnea (a condition in which a person stops breathing while he or she is sleeping) often go to an otolaryngologist. For example, I consult a patient, Jay, with this problem and suspect that a large part of the problem is due to a lower jaw that is abnormally developed and poorly positioned. In addition, while Jay does not realize that the jaw problem is related to the snoring, he admits that this has bothered him cosmetically during the past decade. I refer Jay to the oral surgeon, who is able to surgically correct the deformity both from a functional and cosmetic aspect. After all the necessary investigations and opinions, Jay decides to proceed with the surgery. He is in the hospital for a couple of days after the surgery and all his care is managed by the oral surgeon. Many people do not realize that dentists can function in this capacity.

In the end I had a happy patient who was sleeping better and was more confident about his appearance. Jay's success was largely due to the collaboration of the different professionals who came up with the best management plan unique for him. This example demonstrates how much the two professions overlap with similar interests, concerns, office dynamics, and most importantly for the benefit of the patient.

2.4 Dietetics

A dietitian has many options for choice of practice once training is complete, including working independently in an office setting. The person might also choose to be based in a hospital, or in an environment with other healthcare providers, such as an endocrinologist (i.e., one who specializes in diabetes), a lipidologist (i.e., specializes in patients with raised cholesterol), or a weight-reduction clinic.

The term "nutritionist" is also used for someone in a similar profession, but the credentialing and services provided need to be reviewed by the individual seeking care. In some countries only individuals with the appropriate training and certification are permitted to call themselves a dietitian. Just as in other healthcare fields, dietitians can choose to be just as specialized, for example working in pediatric, research, and corporate settings. For more information on the regulations relating to the profession and the scope of practice, refer to the links which are provided in the Resources section on the CD.

2.5 Midwifery

Midwifery is a profession in which a person can have varying responsibilities and independence, depending on choice, where they completed their training, and the location of practice. In many regions, they can practice as independent practitioners, and provide care relating to pregnancy, including prenatal care, delivery, postpartum care, and care relating to breast-feeding. Some midwives also provide primary care to women relating to female-related issues (e.g., birth control, yearly gynecological exams). Many midwives are closely affiliated with a hospital setting, or with other medical professionals such as obstetricians or family doctors.

Most midwives that I have come across have a nursing background, but many do come from other diverse backgrounds unrelated to medicine, before embarking on training in midwifery. During my undergraduate medical training, I was taught and instructed by midwives relating to normal childbirth in the clinical setting.

2.6 Naturopathy

Personally, I am a big believer in vitamins, natural remedies, and consultation with naturopathic doctors when the need arises. Besides personally utilizing these natural routes of care and supplementation, I incorporate it into my practice as much as possible. Naturopathic physicians practice in many ways just like their medical doctor colleagues, and some patients prefer to have a naturopath as their primary care physician.

One example of how I use non-medicated care for my patients as the first line of management is a relatively new type of nasal spray —

seawater. Yes, it is from the ocean and prepared commercially for nasal application. I believe it works great for regular nasal hygiene as well as a sole, or adjunctive maintenance regime, for such problems as nasal bleeding, sinus disorders, and allergies. I have anecdotally heard of many people whose nose and sinus symptoms clear up when they swim in the sea. I know when I swim in the ocean my nose and sinuses seem to clear up, so I was not surprised when I saw seawater on the drugstore shelves for general use.

Obviously, naturopathic doctors are experts in many different conditions and can recommend naturopathic intervention for most disorders to some degree or another. I have referred many a patient to a naturopathic doctor for an opinion, one classic example being a consultation for ringing in the ears (otherwise known as tinnitus). Some naturopathic remedies have been known to be helpful with this condition. While there is often no medical treatment available for tinnitus, some patients have been helped with naturopathic remedies.

While naturopaths can take care of many things, they do not commonly prescribe medication or perform surgery. There are some countries and jurisdictions that permit naturopathic doctors to prescribe medicine, but that is not universal and very much of a dynamic change. They, too, examine patients as do medical doctors, and have a training program that is in many aspects very similar to medical school.

Although naturopaths try to avoid medications as much as possible, I have been referred many patients from naturopathic doctors as well, when they have seen the need for medical or surgical intervention.

Just to demonstrate the forever and rapidly changing scope of the allied health professions, in the area that I practice, very recently a new ruling has come to effect that naturopathic doctors are permitted to prescribe limited medications themselves.

In terms of the naturopathic office environment, things can run in a similar fashion to an office of a primary care medical doctor, and I know several naturopaths who practice in the same office as a medical doctor.

2.7 Nursing

The nursing profession goes hand in hand with medicine, and in many ways the two disciplines need each other to function. The nursing field has expanded in so many exciting ways, from an educational, research, and practice point of view. The duration of training has become longer in many parts of the world and the specialty options are immense.

Some nurses with advanced training and skills choose to set up an independent practice of their own, either alone, with a group of other nurses, or with other health-care providers. These nurses are referred to amongst others as Nurse Practitioners, Advanced Practice Nurses, Advanced Practice Registered Nurses, and Independent Nurse Contractors. In some areas in the United States and in Canada, these advanced nurses can set up their own independent practices, while in other areas they can open independent practices only with physician collaboration. In some states and provinces, the advanced nurses can also prescribe medication, refer patients to specialists, and even admit patients to health-care facilities. Note that not all states and provinces allow advanced nurses to practice independently. For more information talk to your local nursing association.

Clinical nurse practitioners in North America practice in some ways similar to, and together with, medical doctors. For this reason, the office setup of a nurse practitioner has much in common with that of a medical doctor.

While working up in Northern Canada's isolated communities as a visiting doctor, I came across several nurse practitioners who performed amazing work in medically underserviced areas. The nurses take care of the patients, do the necessary examinations, prescribe medications, and work closely with doctors. Nurse practitioners are an evolving profession, becoming more independent in the urban setting too, with different countries and jurisdictions permitting different levels of practice.

I will give you a concrete example of how this profession can function. Patient Zen was an infant in a remote area in Northern Canada who had recurrent ear infections in the first two years of his life. He needed antibiotics periodically, and if the clinical nurse specialist had not been practicing there, the complications as a result of untreated ear infections could have been significant.

One of the consequences of untreated ear infections is a condition known as mastoiditis (i.e., the infection spreading to the bone in the proximity of the ear), something that can usually be avoided by treating ear infections when needed. The nurse practitioner examined Zen's ears and decided each time whether to give an antibiotic or not. When I arrived there for clinics, the nurse arranged for me to see patients that she felt needed further assessment by an ear specialist, and I would decide on the next mode of treatment. In the case of Zen, insertion of small tubes (known as grommets in some countries) into the eardrums was needed. I arranged for this to be done in the closest city that could do this procedure. Thank goodness for the nurse who was working in this community, contributing in a meaningful way to the care of Zen, avoiding untoward medical complications, and initiating the definitive treatment.

At every stage in my career, whether it is in the hospital setting, or outpatient setting, I have worked closely with nurses. Another example would be a family practice clinic where I worked for a few years. The nurse was the first contact, and did the initial screening and questioning of the patient. She also did part of the basic examination needed for any assessment including the measurement of the pulse, blood pressure, and body temperature. The nurse would give the injections and draw blood for investigations. She would accompany me and help out with some examinations and treatment that were carried out in the examination room. The nurse was a team member every step of the way.

2.8 Occupational therapy

An occupational therapist works closely with physicians and other health-care providers in creating rehabilitation plans for patients, amongst other things. The patients could be in the hospital after a stroke or recuperating at home following a motor vehicle accident. It's an exciting field that people generally know little about.

The training overlaps with medicine in much of what is learned and trained, and there is a strong collaboration with doctors and other health-care providers on many levels. While many occupational therapists work in a hospital, or other health-care facility, they could certainly work independently in an office environment, the function being somewhat similar to any other medical office.

2.9 Optometry

Optometrists also have a doctor designation in many parts of the world. They usually practice independently in an office setting, or they may be closely affiliated to medical doctors — particularly ophthalmologists working in a medical office, or in the hospital.

A while back I personally consulted with an ophthalmologist, the basic eye assessment and examination being performed by an optometrist. I have also seen cross referrals between the two specialties. An ophthalmologist might choose to ask an optometrist to do the initial evaluation of patients before medical treatment is considered, as was the case in my experience. In turn, the optometrist can refer patients to the ophthalmologist for more complex examinations or treatment.

There are limitations with what optometrists can do with many eye disorders. Optometrists do not perform surgery and have limitations in regards to prescribing medication. They do, however, take care of eyes with appropriate examinations, diagnose pathology, and prescribe glasses and contact lenses.

Obviously, as with any of the health-care disciplines, regulations and boundaries of what the scope of practice of optometrists can entail changes from one country, state, or province to the next. Certainly the running of the office has a lot in common with any other medical-related office, but like their ophthalmologist colleagues, the equipment and initial financial outlay far exceeds what most health-care professionals have to spend to get things up and running.

Note that an optometrist is not the same as an optician, although in some countries there is some overlap between these two professions. Opticians deal more with fitting of lenses, and have a wealth of knowledge and information as to the best options for a person's glasses or contact lens prescription.

2.10 Osteopathy

While attending a course on the temporal bone at the House Ear Institute in Los Angeles many years ago, I first came across osteopathic doctors in my professional career. The temporal bone is part of the inner portion of the ear, and the surgery can be quite complex and difficult. It is not always something that can be fully mastered during surgical residency, and it often requires further training.

Osteopathic doctors practice just like medical doctors; for example, they prescribe medicine, do further specialty training, perform surgeries, and take care of patients in a hospital. Their training and practice is somewhat different in that they concentrate on the muscular-skeletal aspect of the body and perform procedures such as spinal manipulations — something that medical doctors do not usually do.

An office for osteopathic doctors would, for the most part, seem exactly the same as medical doctors and patients might never be able to tell the difference in how the two professions function.

2.11 Physiotherapy

Physiotherapy is well known to most people, especially those of us who have had some sort of sports-related injury. These health-care professionals are involved with the muscular-skeletal system — maintenance, diagnosis, and treatment. They can work in a solo or physiotherapy group environment, together with a multi-specialty office, or work full time in a hospital-type environment.

The set up of a physiotherapy office can be quite costly as there are usually expensive purchases needed; for example, some offices provide fitness equipment in a gymnasium setup and maybe even a swimming pool or steam bath.

2.12 Podiatry

It is often very difficult to tell the difference between a podiatrist and medical doctors who specialize in disorders of the foot. Podiatric physicians undergo training similar to medical doctors, but their schooling is more focused on feet. They perform many procedures on nails, toes, and feet including some surgical procedures, which are performed by surgeons as well, particularly orthopedic surgeons.

Podiatrists usually practice in an office setting, most procedures are performed on outpatients. The set up and running of a podiatric office would be indistinguishable from a medical office.

2.13 Psychology

Psychology is a field that people usually know something about, with little explanation needed. What is less well known is that there are many different types of psychologists, besides the clinical psychologist. Industrial, educational, developmental, sports, and forensic psychologists are a few examples of the different types of professionals in this field.

A psychologist's office is certainly simpler to get set up as clinical procedures are not relevant here, but all the same basic principles for office set-up apply.

2.14 Respiratory therapy

Respiratory therapists are integral team members in many hospital settings, and they might also work in selected outpatient facilities independently. They can work on hospital wards, in emergency and operating rooms, or in intensive care units — or more commonly a combination of any of these. They can do specialized diagnostic procedures, administer oxygen, and intubate patients, to name a few of the responsibilities.

A respiratory therapist can certainly work exclusively in the outpatient setting, if this is the choice of the individual. Practice scope could include pulmonary function testing, sleep apnea management, and distribution of other respiratory assistance devices. I personally refer patients for some basic investigations to respiratory therapists.

2.15 Speech-language pathology

Speech-language pathologists are otherwise known as "speech therapists." These health-care providers specialize in speech disorders, voice care, and even swallowing problems. The type of conditions and people they take care of include speech delay, stuttering, singers with poor voice technique, and stroke patients with speech and swallowing issues.

These professionals have a choice as to how they wish to practice. Similar to so many of the other health-care fields, they can work exclusively in the hospital environment, but many choose to have their own office and function independently in their clinical areas of choice, and based on their expertise. The office setup in these situations would be similar to that of other primary health-care providers.

A lot of the time, speech-language pathology is clumped together with audiology. This is a common association in many parts of the world, particularly when it comes to educational institutions and societies.

2.16 Veterinary medicine

For some reason, veterinarians get left out of the picture when the topic of health-care providers or allied health professionals comes up. In many ways, their practice is much more similar to medical and osteopathic doctors than some of the other health-care providers mentioned in the previous sections.

Veterinarians cover a full range of medical services to a variety of "patients," prescribe medications, administer anesthetics, and perform complex surgery. Certainly the office setup can be very complex based on all the functions they perform, but there are many commonalities to the basic principles relating to office dynamics.

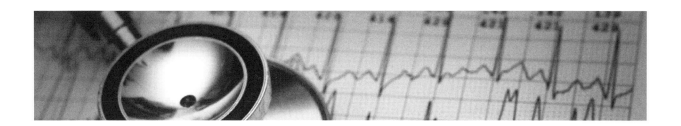

2

IS THE HEALTH-CARE FIELD
THE RIGHT CHOICE FOR YOU?

I can't emphasize enough that whatever stage of the medical career path you are at, nobody will really be happy with what you are doing if you have not gone into a medical career for the right reasons.

While many readers of this book will already be done with medical school and residency, others might just be thinking of applying to medical school, or to one of the allied health profession schools. It is for this reason that I am including some basic concepts to follow. If you are already in the profession, it is not a bad idea to reflect on your own personal reasons for being in your position.

While there is no ideal or perfect personality match for a career in the medical field, being aware of some of the characteristics that are compatible with the profession is vital. People might try and impart their own views about what type of person makes a good doctor or health-care professional, or who should become a doctor — do not buy into this. There is so much diversity is this career and a "cookie-cutter" type personality being the best for the job is just not the case. Having said that, there are clearly characteristics outlined in this chapter that are key to making the right decision about a career in medicine; just keep them in mind. It is all about being appropriately informed and aware of the big picture, before you embark on a career in medicine or any of the other health-care fields.

1. GOOD REASONS FOR CHOOSING A HEALTH-RELATED PROFESSION

This section outlines some of the good reasons to choose to be in a health-related profession.

1.1 You are a caregiver

As a caregiver, you get to care for your fellow human beings. From the time a person first steps into your office, into the hospital, into the operating room, or a specimen arrives at the laboratory, you are on the road to helping someone. This help can make a big change in someone's life, as well as the lives of those around the person.

For example, let's say your first patient of the day walks into your office with a severe sore throat. This person has come to you for help because he or she is unwell and has tried all the measures he or she can to make the situation better. You take a throat swab that turns out to be positive for a bacterial infection of the throat (i.e., strep throat). You prescribe a course of antibiotics, and within 48 hours the patient is much better, back at school and on the football field. The patient phones your office two days later and thanks you, as he or she is feeling much better. How rewarding is that? This is just one example of how you can make a change in another person's life.

Medicine is all about taking care of people. This can occur in a myriad of ways, both directly and indirectly. No matter what field you choose, it will ultimately be about taking care of a patient. On the one end of the spectrum you might have the clinician who cares for, and about, his or her patients on a daily basis. On the other end of the spectrum you can have the clinician scientist, or pathologist, who cares about patients in a very different manner. Neither of these disciplines cares any more, or any less, about their patients, but rather cares for them in different ways.

Some of my mentors and role models, whom I can think back on, imprinted very specific characteristics relating to how I practice today. The most outstanding common feature is the way they cared for their patients, as well

as others around them. To give you one example, I remember one particular surgeon during my residency training days that made an extra effort to make sure parents felt comfortable with any, and all, aspects of their child's care. He really listened and made the parents feel like their child's treatment was the most important thing that was going on at that very moment in time. Spending just a few extra minutes to make sure the parents were more comfortable meant the world to them and it was clearly evident.

For those who might be less caring, situations can come up in which a feeling of discomfort and anxiety on the patient's part can arise, maybe even some animosity. Not only can this have an impact on the patient, but also on the physicians and any of the other people involved in the care of this patient. Negative energy has a domino effect — a health professional's emotions can have implications on those around him or her. If you look at all the different allied health care fields mentioned earlier in the book, this concept can be applied to all of them.

1.2 Exciting

How much more exciting can it get than saving a person's life? Picture yourself walking into an emergency room and seeing a young child gasping for air and unable to breathe. This young patient was eating a big candy and was given a fright by a friend, resulting in the candy being suddenly lodged in the child's throat. I was actually on call once when this very scenario occurred and I was called immediately to the emergency room. Luckily enough, I was not far from the emergency room and was taking a short break in between surgeries; I was able to rush to the situation in no time.

Once I assessed the problem and saw how potentially grave this situation could be, I rushed the patient to the operating room. Due to the position of the candy in the throat, the patient was very fortunate that complete obstruction of the airway did not occur; in other words I had enough time to remove the candy in a more controlled environment and with the appropriate instrumentation. With the help of an anesthesiologist, a careful anesthetic was carried out. Using a steel rigid instrument (laryngoscope) and with a combination of a vacuum device and grasping forceps, the candy was successfully removed. The child woke up from the anesthetic without complication and the parents as well as all health-care parties involved in the care of this patient were ecstatic. Once I had some free time, I ventured back to the emergency room so that I could give feedback to the staff there, and thanked them for their part in the care, and positive outcome, of our mutual patient.

1.3 Rewarding

In the situation of a patient with cancer, it can obviously be very traumatic for all involved — especially the family, but the medical staff too. I can remember one child coming to the hospital very ill with fevers, loss of weight, and a recent history of bruising easily. After several investigations, which were all done on that day in the professional building where the doctor's office was located, he was sent to the local hospital. All of this occurred because the family doctor was very concerned about some type of blood cancer. After the appropriate history and clinical examination in the emergency room, the child underwent an urgent bone marrow biopsy, in order to send some of the aspirate for analysis. A diagnosis of leukemia was made on that same day. As the patient was already in the hospital, he was started on chemotherapy. All of this happened within 24 hours.

Chemotherapy can be a very difficult time for the patient as there are many side effects. Also, there is no guarantee that a patient will be cured and will subsequently survive. I was doing pediatric training at the time and was able to follow this particular patient through the entire treatment phase. Fortunately, this patient responded well to chemotherapy and was cleared of the blood cancer, at least for the short term, and maybe forever. Seeing the patient almost on a deathbed in the emergency room and then seeing a healthy child walk out of the hospital is an amazing experience. This is just one example of how rewarding a career in medicine can be.

1.4 You want to help people

I believe the BOAT concept — an acronym I devised — is the key to success for a happy career in medicine, particularity relating to job satisfaction. I believe it covers what I see as a fundamental concept for choosing a career in a health-care profession — not just wanting to help people, but an *unconditional desire* to help people.

1.4a "B" — unconditional desire to help people despite the "background" of the patient

You often cannot choose who your patients will be and what their background is. I always like to give the example of training or working in an inner-city hospital. The patients that arrive at the doorstep might be far from what you envisioned when you chose medicine as your career. You might find a patient with poor personal hygiene who is combative and rather abusive, verbally. This could be further complicated by a lack of ability for adequate history taking, making for diagnostic challenges. While this might not be a desirable situation for many people working in the medical field, there are just as many health-care professionals who prefer to work in this kind of environment. The level of satisfaction that can be gained from helping people in these deplorable situations can be immense.

You might also have strong religious beliefs and have a patient who lives a lifestyle that fundamentally conflicts with your personal beliefs, morals, and ideals. As a doctor, you cannot impose your own values on a patient. You have to be impartial when treating a patient. There are a few situations in which you might defer the treatment to a colleague if you feel uncomfortable with the situation at hand. Performing abortions is one such example. In my opinion, nobody should be forced to perform abortions, and conversely nobody should be denied a legal abortion because of a doctor's personal beliefs.

1.4b "O" — unconditional desire to help people despite the "outcome" of the patient

Imagine going into medicine thinking that you are always going to be able to make people better? This is often not the case. Picture yourself taking care of the medical needs of a family — a mom, a dad, and two children. The one child is nine years of age, doing well at school, an aspiring figure skater, and already thinking of doing some future humanitarian work at this young age. Very suddenly, the child starts having seizures, never having had a medical problem in the past. After all the necessary investigations, an aggressive brain tumor is diagnosed. This is obviously devastating for all. Despite having all the latest treatments available, including advanced surgery, the child deteriorates, and ultimately dies. Although you can be certain you tried your best, including acquiring the help of colleagues, you have no control of the final outcome — something you have to be aware of, and be able to deal with.

Another patient of yours, a healthy middle-aged man, has elective surgery on his sinuses. During the anesthetic, there is a significant complication as a result of the patient's previously undetected raised blood pressure. His past blood pressure readings appeared to be within normal limits. As a result, under anesthetic he is given medication to lower the blood pressure. This results in a chain of events, ultimately causing a stroke. The patient wakes up with significant impairments, including memory loss and some long-term consequences. Who would have thought that this would have happened to one of your patients? This is certainly an outcome no doctor would have wanted.

1.4c "A" — unconditional desire to help people despite their "appreciation" level

You have to want to help patients because that is something you truly want to do, without the expectation of any kind of appreciation in return. So let's imagine you in this position:

You are a family physician working in a small rural community. There is one hospital in town, and you are covering the Emergency Room (ER) for the night. While attending a birthday celebration for one of your children, you are called urgently to the ER to attend to a passenger injured in a motor vehicle accident. You arrive at the ER to find a young woman lying in a neck brace, speaking appropriately and moving all her limbs. You investigate for many things over the next three hours, including a possible neck injury. In this case you decide the patient is stable enough to stay in the local hospital overnight.

You talk to the patient's family to give them an update of the situation. More family members have arrived, and you now have about ten people staring you in the face and looking rather worried, which is totally understandable. If this was my sister, mother, or friend I would be worried too. While you try to tell them what is going on, they seem frustrated that you do not have more specific answers as to the exact nature of the patient's injuries. The family also expresses concern about why you are taking care of this patient in the local hospital, and have not transferred her to the "big city hospital." During all of this conversation, nobody has acknowledged that you have just spent three hours trying to figure out what's going on with the patient, and little do they know that you left your own child's birthday party to attend to their family member so compassionately and diligently. Up until now, none of the family has said the words "thank you."

Such a situation might be upsetting for some doctors, particularly early on in their career. However, you have to understand that this family is under a lot of stress over their wife, mother, daughter, and sister being in an accident, with the exact nature of her injuries still to be confirmed. Appreciation on the part of patients and/or their loved ones might not be in the equation, at least in the short term, and you have to be fully aware of this concept before you go into medicine. There are different areas in medicine in which similar situations occur.

Don't get me wrong — many patients appreciate what you do, but every now and again this type of situation occurs. Every doctor has his or her own story and personal take on this. So, choose medicine because you want to help people, and not because you want to receive gratitude and recognition for it. This concept is not unique to medicine, but can be of relevance to some of the other health-care fields as well.

1.4d "T" — unconditional desire to help people despite the "treats"

Together with money and status often comes other types of materialistic gain. I am sure you have all come across people who joke about doctors having fancy homes, sports cars, boats, or holiday homes. While sometimes this is the case, I think it's accurate to say most medical doctors do not fall into this category.

If you are thinking of doing medicine and you have thoughts of luxuries as a major motivating factor, you are in for an unpleasant surprise. Often they don't come, and then you will be a doctor without your "treats," and unhappy in your career, which is not a good situation.

1.5 You are dedicated

I cannot think of anyone who has entered a medical field without showing enormous dedication. Achieving the grades and other requirements for acceptance into medical school clearly demonstrates dedication and determination. In order for you to proceed successfully in this career, these qualities are definitely required. There is no area of the health-care fields in which you do not need commitment in order to go forward and succeed.

Let me give you an example of how dedication can clearly be displayed by a person. Let's call this person Joe for the sake of the illustration.

Joe always wanted to be a doctor from as young as he can remember. He is also a star athlete, ice hockey being his strongest sport. Joe, while having the ability to excel in the ice hockey world, has decided to pursue his life-long dream of becoming a medical doctor. Due to the enormous amount of time spent on hockey training, Joe's grades are not fantastic, but they are good enough to apply to medical school.

Joe applies to five medical schools and does not even get an interview at any of them. He decides to do a year of basic science courses to prove that that he is able to excel academically. The next year, Joe applies to four medical schools and gets an interview at three of them. Unfortunately, when it comes to final selection, he is rejected at all three schools — the competition is just too tough. Judging by information provided by the universities and the available statistics, he suspects his performance in the interview process brought him down. Joe is determined to continue the challenge to go to medical school. He is also becoming more and more in debt from the years of study, and only being able to work part time. His hockey is now limited to a community league, as he does not have the time to play on a more serious level.

Joe spends the next year doing a few more courses and volunteering on a project for a clinician scientist, as well as volunteering in an emergency department at the local hospital. He knows that these things will also strengthen his application. During this time he tries to practice interviewing techniques as much as he can, but he finds it tough to find interview partners. Joe then applies for the third time to five medical schools. He gets an interview at all of them and receives an acceptance offer from two of them. Dedication has finally paid off!

This type of situation is not that uncommon among medical school applicants. Determined applicants will not give up their goal of ultimately getting that acceptance letter.

1.6 You are patient

It is funny to me that being "patient," and taking care of a "patient" have the same word in common. According to *Longman English Dictionary*, "patient" as a noun means: "someone who is receiving medical treatment from a doctor or in a hospital." As a verb, "patient" means "able to wait calmly for a long time or to accept difficulties, people's annoying behavior, etc., without becoming angry." While every dictionary you consult will have a different interpretation of the word, I feel these definitions are very appropriate in the medical context.

It is very important to have patience all along the way. From the outset of your journey toward becoming a medical professional, during further training, while setting up your office, practicing as a doctor and beyond, you will need patience. Life will become very difficult for all involved if you are unreasonably impatient. I use the word "unreasonably" as most people have some form of impatience to varying degrees.

I believe not having sufficient patience will impact on your ability to be happy in this career. For example, picture a family doctor (general practitioner), Dr. Smith, who has practiced medicine for ten years. While inherently being a somewhat impatient individual, Dr. Smith has managed to keep things seemingly under control up until this point.

The situation, however, has now become more difficult. Dr. Smith has a busy and successful practice, seeing about 40 patients a day, which is a lot. He is having difficulty taking the time to listen to the patients like he once did. He seems to cut them off quicker, sometimes even mid-sentence, while they are describing their symptoms to him. He becomes more abrupt with his responses, and lacks the necessary sensitivity that he used to have. At the end of most patient visits, Dr. Smith is standing with his hand on the door handle before the patient is fully content with his explanations, or feeling ready to leave the room. He never used to be like this. This does not make for a happy day in the office, nor does it make for a satisfying or content feeling on the part of the patient.

While there could be many reasons for a doctor developing this type of practice behavior, one would hate to think that this is the result of increasing frustration with a career choice and an acquired intolerance for spending time with patients. You can only hide your true self for so long, and showing your dissatisfaction with a career in medicine is no exception. While this might be something that surreptitiously snuck up during the years, there are things you can do to try and improve the situation. Seeing 40 patients a day is draining for anyone, and simply modifying the schedule and seeing less patients can do wonders for some people.

2. THE WRONG REASONS TO CHOOSE A HEALTH-RELATED PROFESSION

The following sections outline some of the wrong reasons on which to base your decision to become a health-care professional.

2.1 Family pressure

The time has come for choosing that career path toward the end of high school. You are very smart and obtaining stellar grades; you are especially strong in the basic sciences. In addition to your academic strengths, you are a gifted piano player and vocalist. You have spent almost every spare minute you have on the piano, singing and compiling your own jazz tunes. You have already done the basic piano training and vocal coaching and are now able to continue playing, singing, and composing music independently. You have starred in every school musical produced at the schools that you have attended in the past ten years. You wanted to join a band, but being 17 years of age, your parents have put on the brakes and said you have to concentrate more on getting into medical school. You certainly have a strong interest in medicine, but you are clearly very musically talented and that is all you really want to do!

Both your parents are academics, one in the area of mechanical engineering and the other in human anatomy. While your interests in going to medical school are known to your parents, your love of music and talents are even better known. Both your parents have always drummed into you that medicine would be the better option, as it is a much safer route for a career than music.

In addition, your favorite grandmother has instilled into you that the need to be a successful professional is paramount. Both she and your grandfather came from Europe to North America with small children and little money. They had to start from scratch with trades and hard labor to survive and support the family. They struggled and sacrificed in so many different ways so that they could give their children and grandchildren the opportunities that they did not have themselves. Your grandmother really wants you become a doctor and you certainly have the smarts and grades to do it.

While you really want to pursue your dreams and passion to be a full-time musician, you cave into family pressure and apply to medical school. Deep inside you wish you were not accepted, but as you are an outstanding candidate, you easily secure one of those coveted positions that are so treasured and sought after by many. You concede that medicine is not so bad after all, as it is a well-paid and respected profession. Of even more importance to you is the fact that you have made your parents very happy. The person most thrilled is your grandmother, who tears up every time she thinks of the concept that her grandchild is about to enter medical school and become a medical doctor. Finally, she feels her sacrifices in life have paid off.

This is not a good situation, and not a reason for going into medicine. While you might ultimately enjoy a career in medicine, there is a good chance that you will not be happy with your choice and will always think about your passion for music and "what if?" It should be emphasized at this point that medicine and the arts are very compatible and I know many physicians who are very talented and successful musicians while being physicians at the same time. There does, however, have to be a strong inherent desire to be a doctor before you embark on a career in medicine.

I actually remember vividly one essay that was written by an applicant to medical school. A file reviewer read it out aloud to the selection committee. This essay was incredibly well written and the applicant explained his love for music in enormous detail. Most of the essay revolved around his musical accomplishments and there was little to hear about a true desire to be a medical doctor. It was almost as if he was telling us — please don't accept me, because I really want to follow my dreams to be a musician. This candidate did not get accepted into the program and, as I said earlier in the book, some things are just meant to be!

2.2 Money

As mentioned earlier, many people in the general public believe being a medical doctor is synonymous with being rich — but this is not always the case. Certainly doctors are in the upper-income bracket for earning potential, but there are easier ways to make money. Not everyone in medicine has the money they would have liked or thought they would have had. Money should not be a primary motivating factor for doing medicine.

Let me give you an example to further outline this point. You are a man who has just finished a public-health specialty-training program. During the course of your training program, your family has expanded in size and you now have two small kids — both children are younger than the age of three. You and

your wife have decided that she is going to stay home for now and be there for the upbringing of the children — childcare during the day was the alternative and you have collectively decided against this. Your wife was working as a dental hygienist for two years and was significantly contributing to the income of the family. You have a hefty student loan and are carrying a balance on two credit cards.

A dream job has just become available for a junior medical officer in a government-based, public-health agency. While the salary is a lot more money than you have ever earned, it is a far cry from the big bucks your friend, who started working a couple years earlier as a family physician in private practice, is making. In fact, your high school friend who has a successful plumbing business is way ahead of both you and your family practice friend in terms of finances and comfort.

You and your wife decide that you are going to pursue this job of your dreams and continue living within your means and not increasing your debt load any further. You stay in your rented apartment for now, do not get a second car, and start to slowly pay off the loans and clear the credit card balances while working in this modest-paid position.

Realistically, it might be another few years before you can buy your own home and go on some exotic vacation. However, these material things are less important as all involved seem to be content with how things have transpired. You are happy going to work every day, and that joy is evident in your personal and professional life. This shows that money has been a secondary issue all along.

However, if you have entered into this career path to make lots of money, a situation like this will be extremely frustrating for you. Even worse, if you have chosen another area in the medical field in which a higher income is possible, and chosen it just for the sake of making more money, then you are likely well on your way to a miserable and unfulfilled career.

2.3 Status

You have always wanted to be physician because doctors are apparently so well respected. You cannot wait until the day you can tell everyone you are a medical student and later a fully qualified medical doctor, maybe even a brain surgeon! These superficial concepts far outweigh your inherent desire to help people. Actually you have a long-standing passion for flying and wish to become a pilot one day, even if it means doing it in your spare time when you are not in the medical office.

You eventually get to display that stethoscope in your pocket and around your neck every chance you get. Somehow you wonder how that novelty of the stethoscope being visible at all times could ever wear off. Well something happened, because after a few years in medical school, the joy of showing off the stethoscope has waned. This is because the motives and primary reasons for following a career in medicine were very wrong.

Another factor could be somehow feeling special when you are paged, or called, to the emergency department at the hospital. This makes you feel especially important and special while amongst other people, or at some social event. The novelty of been called away from the office, home, a family function, or a social event wears off very quickly. People in this situation often wonder how on earth they ever got themselves into this in the first place.

If the reasons for choosing medicine were honest and true to yourself, when things get tough, the stress will be that much easier to deal with as you will hopefully really enjoy what you are doing. No job is void of stress, and all careers have less desirable portions. What is important is that you enjoy more aspects of your job than you dislike.

3. THERE ARE MANY DIFFERENT SPECIALTIES FROM WHICH TO CHOOSE

Some people have decided early on in their lives that they want follow a certain specialty. Others make that decision during university, or even beyond. Irrespective of when you make that ultimate decision, you have a multitude of specialties from which to choose.

Sometimes it is really difficult to find that niche that suits you, but it is important you make the right decision. It is crucial to experience, or be aware of the vast selection of specialty training before you decide.

In the earlier years of medical school, you have exposure to the main fields in medicine — pediatrics and general surgery being two examples. The more specialized areas of medicine usually come later on in your training, for example, during elective time. Such areas include specialties to the likes of pediatric cardiovascular surgery and medical genetics.

In some countries, certainly in the United States and Canada, there is more pressure these days to make an important decision about a specialty earlier on, before you have had an opportunity to finish medical school or before you have any experience in practicing general medicine. While most individuals make the decision to specialize during medical school, there are always ways you can further specialize later on in your career. Keep your eyes and ears open from an early stage, even before entering medical school, in order to be aware of as many of the different areas of medicine as possible. Exposure is key to ultimately being in a good position to make a decision.

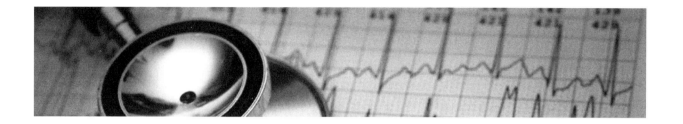

3

IMPORTANT INFORMATION TO KNOW BEFORE YOU BEGIN

Working in a health-care profession has many differences from other careers such as it is much more regulated with licensing and registration requirements. Some states and provinces also require physicians to take courses each year to expand and improve their skills. There are also many different types of review boards that people in the health-care fields have to deal with. This chapter will help make you aware of these types of situations.

1. LICENSING, REGISTRATION, AND MEMBERSHIP

There are many steps to complete, and standards to comply with, before you get your license to practice. Being able to practice does not necessarily mean setting out the shingle once you have completed the marathon amount of training and successfully passed the exams. There is so much variance in this process depending on the health-care discipline, geographic location, and more. The best way to demonstrate this would be to give you a few examples to provide you with a taste of how complex this concept can be.

Dr. Andy has just finished his two-year family practice residency in Canada, which was preceded by four years of medical school. For the first time, he can be licensed with the provincial College of Physicians and Surgeons as an independent practitioner. Dr. Andy has also met all the requirements and has passed his certification exams for the Family Practice specialty certification and is now able to use the designation CCFP (Certificant of the College of Family Physicians of Canada) after his MD (Doctor of Medicine), at the end of his signature.

Dr. Space recently graduated as a general surgeon in California. She has passed her board certification exams and has license to practice surgery in the State of California (from the Medical Board of California). Besides her MD designation, she would also like to obtain the FACS (Fellow of the American College of Surgeons) designation. In order to obtain this designation, there are many requirements that have to be met. One such requirement is completing at least one year of surgical practice after completion of all formal training. Dr. Space has to wait a while before being eligible for this professional affiliation and designation.

There are multiple organizations in many of the health-related fields that you can have a membership with, each with their own unique requirement for membership and related fees.

I will provide you with a few examples of the societies and memberships that are available in the fields in which I work. They will give you some idea how broad the scope can be (these exclude licensing bodies, insurance affiliations, and alumni organizations):

- Canadian Medical Association
- Canadian Pediatric Society
- American Academy of Pediatrics
- Canadian Society of Otolaryngology/ Head and Neck Surgery
- American Academy of Otolaryngology/ Head and Neck Surgery
- British Columbia Medical Association
- British Columbia Pediatric Society
- British Columbia Otolaryngology Society
- Triological Society

While it would be ideal to be a member and enjoy the benefits of many organizations, you have to be selective in terms of membership as you can find yourself spending a lot of money on all the yearly fees. Some memberships are more costly than others, and some are more important for you to be a part of than others. This is obviously dependent on the health profession you are in, but most fields have a vast array of organizations of direct relevance to the practice, so you will have to be selective. With some health-care fields you can literally spend thousands of dollars per annum on memberships.

I was more inclusive with my memberships earlier on in my career, and then dropped the memberships that I felt were of least relevance and benefit to my personal practice situation. My advice to you, particularly if you are starting up in your career and practice, is to be part of as many societies relevant to your clinical domain as you can afford, and then decide later (even after one year) which memberships you wish to continue.

2. CONTINUING MEDICAL EDUCATION

Continuing Medical Education (CME) is the eternal learning process that is an integral part of any health professional's existence. There are always new things to learn in medicine, and knowledge to update and review. This term is common to most health-care professions, but other terms are also used including Continuing Professional Development (CPD).

While many health professionals do this because they want to do it, some doctors are required to do continuing medical education for maintenance of knowledge, skills, or certification. There is usually a minimum amount of hours that are necessary in order to meet these requirements. There might also be guidelines as to the type of educational activity, or level of engagement, that is optimal for this ongoing education — this all depends on the jurisdiction, or country, with which you are working or affiliated.

There are so many different forums in which this learning can take place. Examples include conventions, conferences, group learning, medical rounds, and even web-based learning. The learning can take place in your hometown, at some coastal resort, or even aboard a cruise ship! There are structured programs for all the different specialties in these locations and venues. In order that educational credits can be obtained from these learning events, these programs usually require some endorsement or approval from an educational organization that deems these experiences eligible as suitable learning and time well spent. Continuing medical education has been an important part of my career, both as the student as well as an educator in the same field.

For many health-care professionals, CME is tax-deductible, or at least partially deductible. This, once again, depends on the location of your practice and the type of setup you have. Certainly in many parts of the world, being in an office setting would be in keeping with being self-employed and/or incorporated. There would thus be opportunities for you to learn while incorporating a tax benefit at the same time. Some venues might be acceptable for tax-deduction purposes, while others would not be.

There are also guidelines as to how much you can deduct — you cannot claim two-weeks' travel and accommodation from North America to Australia for a one-day meeting! You also cannot also claim a tax benefit for a meeting that has nothing to do with what you are practicing. Be sure to consult with your accountant about the tax implications of CME. An accountant is a specialist in this area and can help you plan all aspects of your business, particularly what is tax deductible when you set up in practice.

2.1 Additional Learning

Those who are interested in a medical field usually have a curious mind from the outset. It is the type of profession in which curiosity and lifelong learning are important to success and job satisfaction. There is so much exciting medical advancement that it is impossible not to have your curiosity constantly stimulated.

During every stage of the journey there is some knowledge or experience to gain, as medicine is a lifelong learning process. The learning can be as simple as reading a medical journal, to as complex as embarking on a whole new specialty training program.

Reading journals is not the only way to keep up-to-date. There is so much information on the Internet. You might also have patients who bring you information that they have found on the Web, read in newspapers, or saw on TV. In my earlier days in practice, I used to feel intimidated by this, but I soon realized it was impossible for me to know everything out there, particularly about something that aired the previous evening on CNN or CBC!

Imagine being a family physician and then deciding that you would like to develop an interest in advanced skills relating to the field of emergency medicine. While you can choose to do an entire specialty training program in emergency medicine, you can also choose to do an abridged course to gain more knowledge in emergency care. For example, by doing one year of further training, you can go back to your community and do more shifts in the hospital emergency department, or even just feel more comfortable in what you are already doing.

This type of flexibility in further training obviously differs in nature from one country to the next. Certainly in North America there are many family physicians that have done an extra year in emergency medicine and then worked full time in an emergency room setting thereafter. It should be emphasized that there is an entire specialty training program in emergency care, and this abbreviated route is not the same as the lengthy process.

No matter what health profession you choose, diversity in learning and training, or branching out into an area of expertise is always an option. The constant learning process and maintaining up-to-date knowledge, and knowing the available routes for achieving this, is also an integral part of all the health-care professions.

Medical school, or training in one of the other health-care related fields, is a terrific experience to gain more knowledge in your chosen career at the most basic or core level, and the learning curve continues through specialty training and practice. I often think back to the days when I was a medical student. The amount of innovation that was going on relating to the medical field was incredible. Then, during my eight years of residency, I saw all kinds of new diagnostic technology and treatment options. I continue to learn things almost every day in medicine. Modern day advancement in technology relating specifically to medical education is just mind-boggling. For me, there is no dull moment as my curiosity continues to be a big part of my fascination and satisfaction with the medical field.

This learning curve will apply to starting a new practice too — you will learn every day as you become more experienced with what works well, and what works not so well.

3. REVIEWS

A physician can be reviewed on many different levels. Many people just coming into health-care professions, and even at the time of starting up a practice, have no idea how extensive the review process can be. The important task of reviews, which doctors have to undergo periodically, is also less well known to the public. The following sections will give you a few examples of reviews.

3.1 Peer reviews

The peer review is an assessment by a colleague, or team of colleagues, as to whether you are practicing within acceptable standards of practice for the discipline and profession. Usually these reviews are random, but they might be as a result of a "red flag" that has come to the attention of a licensing office or funding agency.

The peer review team can come and take a careful look at your office, review your records, and examine your equipment. They can also assess your methods of sterilization, and basically do anything that they think is relevant to assess the level of care.

While many might see this as intimidating, it is supposed to be an educational experience to see if there are any ways you can improve your practice of medicine, evaluated by your very own colleagues who are familiar with your type of practice. Ultimately, these types of interventions are in place to protect the public and to make sure everyone is meeting the highest standards of patient care.

This type of quality control is not limited to medical doctors, as many other health professions use it as well.

3.2 Billing reviews

A billing review usually occurs when doctors bill for services rendered, either to an insurance company or government funding authority. This can be a random check, or a process stimulated by an alert from one of these funding agencies to your college or public funding source.

In Canada, for example, physicians are mostly funded through a provincial government-funding source. If a discrepancy in billing practices comes to the attention of the organization, it will initiate a review.

This type of check is in place to make sure physicians' billing practices are accurate and representative of services provided. There are many different ways such a review can be carried out. The billing authority might contact your patients directly confirming a certain visit, or treatment, that was billed and paid for. This could also involve asking the doctor to provide documentation, or proof, for services billed.

Unfortunately, there are situations in which doctors might unintentionally, or even intentionally, incorrectly bill for services not provided, or modify the level of treatment actually carried out. Doctors are occasionally found to be committing fraud with billing practices; the consequences of such a deplorable act vary.

This practice of billing reviews naturally applies to other health-care fields, each with their own way of assessing and managing the situation.

3.3 Licensing body review

A country, state, or provincial authority might be able to review your practice if the need arises. An example of this need could be a report of unprofessional behavior with a patient, which could even result in a criminal investigation.

4. PROFESSIONALISM

Professionalism is a broad concept that has so many different interpretations. If you speak to doctors, community members, educators, and others, each person will come up with his or her own interpretation as to what professionalism actually means and how it relates to the medical profession. The understanding, research, advocacy, and enforcement of this rather controversial area are an ever-evolving process.

While a health-care worker should be professional, there are many interpretations of what professionalism is — it depends on many factors.

Rather than go into all the different interpretations and definitions, let me give you a couple of concrete examples of how professionalism can come in to play with the practice of medicine.

Dr. Uls is a male family physician in his late forties. His female patient, Ms. Nee, is in her twenties and is a fairly new patient in the practice. During the third visit Ms. Nee discloses to Dr. Uls that she has been lonely since moving to the area, and has difficulty meeting new people. This, in turn, is contributing to her depression. In addition to counseling the patient about the depression and discussing the option for medication, Dr. Uls asks the patient if she would like to go out for dinner one night, as he feels sorry for her, being that she is lonely and doesn't know many people in the area. Ms. Nee gladly accepts his offer for dinner and is very excited about the prospect of a night out on the town.

The next week they go out for dinner, and the wine flows freely. At the end of the evening Ms. Nee invites Dr. Uls into her home and he gladly accepts. Later on that evening they become significantly intimate. Their relationship continues for weeks with several dinner dates, the physical aspects of the relationship become more intense too.

After three months of this courtship, things then don't go well for them; Dr. Uls decides it's time to slow things down. Ms. Nee becomes more and more depressed and her medication is not helping any more. She tells a friend about the worsening depression and her relationship with the doctor. The friend (correctly) tells her how wrong this situation is because the doctor is behaving very inappropriately. At the advice of her friend, the patient proceeds with a complaint to the licensing authority responsible for the certification and licensing of the doctor. A comprehensive investigation is undertaken which is painful for all involved. The doctor is found to have behaved unprofessionally and his license is revoked.

This is a clear-cut example of unprofessional behavior. Simply put, a doctor cannot date his or her patients. A patient in a situation like the one described is vulnerable, and does not have the strength, and perhaps judgment, to prevent a scenario like this occurring. It must be mentioned though, that while this might not have been the case here, it may be the patient who makes the initial move. This makes no difference in terms of the conduct of the physician. A physician must refrain from intimate relations with a patient at all times, regardless of who initiates the relationship.

Be aware that there are processes and investigation procedures in place, such as what happened in this example, for the protection of the public. Such procedures are aimed to ensure that the highest professional standards are met, and that the safety of patients and public is maintained.

Another example: Dr. Ells has a busy surgical practice. She has a high-volume practice and sees lots of patients on a daily basis. Dr. Ells generally writes her notes in a file after each patient visit, rather than leaving them all for the end of the day.

For one of the patients who was seen on a specific day, the problem seemed pretty routine and Dr. Ells writes her usual few words saying everything is fine and the post-operative wound looks good. Three months down the road, the doctor receive a letter from a lawyer stating that the patient is suing Dr. Ells for negligence. Dr. Ells manages to obtain some information about the circumstances and finds out that a bad infection was present in this patient after her last visit, and that the patient had one complication after another, resulting in a two-month hospital stay. Dr. Ells goes back and reviews her notes and decides to change the notes for that visit. She adds to the notes that "there might be some early signs of infection and that she discussed the situation with the patient but the patient does not want to go on an antibiotic." The legal case proceeds and it is discovered that the doctor did indeed change her notes after the fact. Dr. Ells is found guilty of altering documentation and, besides the legal ramifications, her license to practice medicine is revoked. She has clearly demonstrated unprofessional behavior and this type of situation is not tolerated in the medical profession.

These are fairly extreme examples of unprofessional behavior, but they really do happen. Note that these examples are modifications of true stories.

There is such a broad spectrum of what can be classified as unprofessional behavior in a health-care profession. It can include things such as the attire worn in the office, racial slurs, and language used with patients.

You do need to keep in mind that professionalism is an ever-evolving area of the health-care professions. The public and governing bodies struggle with specific boundaries and definitions relating to professionalism. To further complicate matters there are cultural differences and sensitivities. What might be acceptable behavior in one culture could be considered unprofessional behavior in another. Most people, however, inherently know what is the right thing to do, and how to behave appropriately.

You just need to surf the Web, particularly medical licensing bodies, and you will find many unprofessional situations described, not unlike the scenarios mentioned in the examples. Transparency is becoming a hallmark when unprofessional behavior has been identified, or disciplinary proceedings undertaken. The public can then be fully aware of all aspects of a physician's credentialing and make informed decisions as to whether they wish to have a certain person as their doctor.

5. PERSONAL SUPPORT

Health-care professionals, like any other members of the public, can have personal problems. The problems may include marital or relationship strife, alcoholism, drug abuse, gambling, mental illness, crime, and more. Often, physicians feel isolated in that they do not want to talk about their issues at all. Times are finally starting to change and people are more comfortable expressing their personal problems, physicians included.

Universities, licensing bodies, and medical societies are making an asserted effort to reach out to physicians and other health-care providers in need of help. There are many different ways that this is undertaken including lectures, seminars, workshops, counseling services, confidential outreach services, and 24-hour phone lines. It is my impression that the new generation of doctors is coming into medicine already speaking more about personal problems and not shying away from this for fear of condemnation or embarrassment. I have seen this in the medical school admissions process where applicants disclose the types of problems they have, including mental illness, before they are even accepted into medical school.

The public, especially in smaller communities, has traditionally put health-care professionals on a pedestal. I believe that notion is slowly starting to fade as people understand, and appreciate, that doctors, nurses, dentists, and other health-care providers are just like everyone else, especially when it comes to the problems that everyone faces in everyday life situations.

It cannot be emphasized enough that there are personal support networks offered to health professionals through their unions, associations, and other organizations. If the need arises, people in the medical field and allied health professions should not hesitate to use these services.

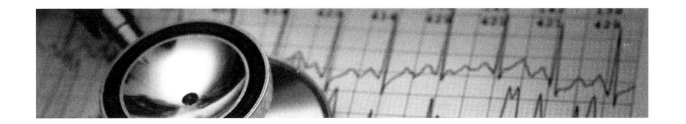

4

CHOOSING THE TYPE OF OFFICE PRACTICE

I have had experience in all of the practice opportunities discussed in this chapter. Each style of practice has its own pros and cons. There is no perfect situation, but it's most important to be in an environment that best suits your needs and personality, and meets the local demand for your services. Being in a situation that does not fit you well will lead to problems in some way or another. As is the case for most aspects of this book, some of these practice opportunities are applicable to all the health-care professions.

As you read through each section you may want to consider the following questions:

- Do you have the motivation to run your own business?

- Do you have an adequate amount of time to spend at this point in your career in setting up a new office?

- Can you do the research that it takes to start a business?

- Are you prepared financially to start a solo practice or will you need a partner to help with the start-up costs?

- Are you capable of being your own boss and making tough decisions?

- Do you think you need colleagues in close vicinity to be able to consult with, or are you ready to be somewhat isolated in your own practice?

1. SOLO PRACTICE

My experience with setting up a solo practice and being in this environment was a most enjoyable and rewarding time in my career. I got to make all the decisions, hire the staff I wanted to hire, make my own office hours, and figure out how to run things myself.

While this might all sound fine, there are downsides to operating a solo practice. You pay all the expenses yourself with no help from others — that is if you do not have other people working in your office who contribute in some way or other. You also do not have colleagues in your office with whom you can easily collaborate on things, particularly relating to patient management. Instead, it might mean a phone call or two, but it is never the same as "knocking" on the next door to discuss something with one of your colleagues right there and then. The technology boom has certainly made this less of a problem, as advice and information is just a click of a button away on the computer.

For me, the benefits of setting up and running a solo practice far outweighed the downsides and I would recommend it to anyone who prefers to work solo. It definitely requires more work initially, and possibly an element of risk. Work will entail all the steps, checks, and balances along the way to get things going, including the necessary research and a business plan (discussed in Chapter 5).

Potential risk involved is essentially twofold. First, you might be starting this practice from scratch and need to get patient volume and a referral base set up. Unless you walk into a turnkey office with a large patient base already, there is no guarantee the patients will be waiting on your doorstep.

From a financial point of view, there is the obvious initial monetary outlay, including potentially large loans, with no assurance that you are going to be busy enough to cover overhead and other payments, especially in the earlier stages. I do, however, believe that if you are motivated enough, you have done your

research, and you practice good medicine, it will happen despite the challenges.

You will not know everything when you begin, and you are likely going to get advice and many different opinions, but ultimately you will figure things out along the way to best suit your needs and style. Everyone who has set up their own office will have their own unique pearls of wisdom that they are usually eager to share. Ask around in the area — perhaps someone has opened up a similar practice in the recent past. There will undoubtedly be someone in your clinical area that can be a mentor for you.

If other practices in your geographic area do not offer much advice, you might have to look to other sources for information, such as consultants who offer professional services to new office setups. In regard to consultants, I suggest you contact professional associations with which you are affiliated. Most professional associations will have information and contact details for you for such services. Another area to find information is in publications relating to your field, which often have advertisements that offer professional consulting for office setups — be sure to check the classifieds in these medical journals or industry-specific publications.

2. GROUP PRACTICE

Many health-care professionals prefer to work in a group environment. There are many advantages to this type of environment. We have already discussed in the previous section the advantage of having colleagues around to easily bounce ideas off for the benefit of your patients — this privilege should never be underestimated, especially early on in your career.

Another benefit of a group practice, which both you and your patients will benefit from, is having people around to cover your patients when you are away for whatever reason, be it vacations, conferences, or illness. For your patients, it will mean having someone in the office available to consult during your absence, where familiarity and comfort already exists with regard to the staff and environment. Of major convenience is that the patient records, results, etc., are present and available for the stand-in health-care provider to access immediately. If you were in a solo practice, the patients would have to find an alternate provider and the health histories and records would pose obvious challenges in many situations.

With regard to the physician, you can leave the office for a period of time knowing your patients are well cared for. When I was in solo practice, I remember many a time where I had to phone around and ask if another doctor could cover my practice, particularly relating to more acute problems. While there is always an emergency department for your patients to go to, it's best to have someone familiar with your specialty and related problems, particularly if the problem is acute in nature and you are in the middle of a treatment regime. One example that illustrates this well is a post-operative patient. The surgery could have been done three days prior, and require removal of sutures one week after the surgery. It would be best if done by someone who is familiar with the type of surgery done and who has been given a briefing of the situation prior to the visit.

While many of these things might seem straightforward to you, some things will only be discovered once you are up and running in your solo practice, having not been previously given a heads up of the advantages of a group practice.

From an economic standpoint, a group practice always seems to make total sense. Many physicians do not work every day, or all day, in the office. This particularly applies to those who have more than one practice location, have a surgical practice where procedures are regularly performed in a hospital setting, those who cover on-call or shifts on a frequent basis in an acute-care setting, or those who are working part time. Many senior doctors are now opting for reduced work hours rather than not working at all. In these situations, the office might be empty much of the time. Overhead can be steep and paying all this money to only be in the office on a very part-time basis makes no economic sense to many. By optimizing the space utilization and maximizing productivity in the office, this will allow more take-home pay versus channeling large amounts into an underutilized office.

One of the downsides to a group practice is the office and support staff, who have to deal with the extra burden of work, and related stress from multiple health-care professionals, each person with his or her own routine and likes and dislikes. Be sensitive to your staff and what is on their plate. Burnout is something you have to watch for, so keep a close eye on how your staff are doing. Also, making happy, effective staff unhappy by having to deal with different, sometimes challenging personalities will affect the dynamics, as well as possibly cause you to lose a good employee.

If you have decided on a group practice, how do you go about getting the right people together? Well, firstly, there might be no choice in the matter. If you end up in an established office with an already set group of health-care providers, you are going to have to fit in with the group and make it work.

If you have the option as to who you would like to include, then think wisely as to who you would like to have as an addition to your office staff. Sometimes supply and demand will make the situation a little more difficult in that you have less choice in the matter, but sometimes waiting it out and getting the right people will help you that much more in the long term. For example, a family doctor might want to include more family doctors, nurse practitioners, and dietitians, to name a few examples. An ophthalmologist could consider an optometrist or an optician. A chiropractor may want to include a naturopath and massage therapist as part of a wellness clinic. These are just a few of the multitude of combinations that are options for you.

My experience of working in group environments has included clinics and facilities with a combination of primary care physicians, specialists, chiropractors, audiologists, and others. These combinations have always been a positive experience for me in a very collaborative environment. Personality conflicts have certainly not been a problem from my experience, but that is something you should actively be aware of when choosing a group environment. You know yourself and what best works for you, and what type of people you best get on with. I have seen, in some offices, situations that led to a premature split, but in these circumstances the situation was unpredictable, just as in many other life situations.

It should also be known that a group practice involves more work, such as additional administrative duties; frequent meetings being one example. In order to make any business, including a doctor's office run smoothly, involved parties have to get together periodically to make collective decisions and ensure adequate office functioning. While this does happen in a solo practice, particularly if you have several employees, the group practice requires more diligence in this regard. I know one dentist's office, involving a group of dentists, oral hygienists, dental assistants, and administrative office staff, where they meet every morning before the work day begins to discuss the planning for the day to make sure things run smoothly.

Also of significance in a group practice, which could be difficult for many to reason with, is that when you are hiring or firing an employee, it has to be done collectively. In a solo practice you can decide solely as to who you want in your office. So, a lot more collaborative work goes on behind the scenes in a group practice than might meet the eye.

3. ASSOCIATE

The associate office setup, or term, is particularly common in a dentist's office, but is widely popular in all the heath-care fields. These individuals opt to work in an office owned by somebody else, and they practice in this environment under many different conditions and business plans. This might be by significant contribution of office expenses, working on a commission basis, or even being salaried.

The following is an example of an associate setup, but keep in mind that there are a multitude of options:

Dr. Dent is a newly trained dentist who is not ready to begin his own practice. While he would very much like to have his own office one day, this is something that he is not ready to do yet, because he has huge student debt to pay off and doesn't want to increase his debt load. He has found two established dental offices that are willing to take on an associate once or twice week. In the one office Dr. Dent pays a "chair" fee and pays the establishment a set amount for the day. All the money received for services on that day go directly to Dr. Dent. In the other office, he works exclusively on an income-splitting basis whereby all the billings are split evenly between the practice and Dr. Dent.

Whatever the plans for the working conditions in an associate relationship, make sure you do your homework and research the situation before signing on the dotted line. You do not want to be working to make someone else rich when you potentially have other options. Even worse, you do not want to be paying fees or commissions that are totally out of the range of similar setups for your clinical discipline and geographic location.

4. LOCUM TENENS

A locum tenens is a person that temporarily substitutes in a job for another person. The following are examples of locum tenens.

The first example includes Dr. Smith who is a newly trained dermatologist, considering the possibilities for relocation at the outset of his career. He has a partner, and they have been having a long-distance relationship for years. His partner's career is not allowing for her to move, so Dr. Smith has to make some big decisions, as the opportunities in his present location are immense. Before getting committed to a long-term practice where he presently resides, he decides to do a locum to buy time.

Dr. Smith finds Dr. Young, who is a dermatologist who is going on sabbatical to Africa for six months and is looking for somebody to cover his practice for this period. Dr. Smith feels this is the perfect opportunity, allowing him some time to decide if moving is the right decision. He agrees to work as locum tenens for a six-month period. After some discussion, they come to a financial agreement whereby Dr. Smith pays Dr. Young a set amount per month to cover expenses, and all the billings go directly to Dr. Smith.

After the six months is completed, Dr. Smith decides that relocating to be with his partner is the right decision, and he packs up and goes without any commitments or obligations — this, of course, was preceded by a position being secured in the new location.

The second example involves Dr. Wright, a physician who is mid-career and has decided to concentrate more on academic medicine versus clinical practice. She sells her practice and works almost full time at the university. She does, however, wish to maintain her clinical skills and certainly still wants to be involved in taking care of patients.

Dr. Wright manages to find a colleague who has the need for sporadic help in the office, particularly when the other doctors take extended breaks. She works as a locum for this practice, taking care of practice matters at certain times of the year for a limited period of time. As this practice is located in an acute-care hospital, Dr. Wright requires the appropriate privileges in order to work in the clinic, albeit temporary locum work. Locum privileges were arranged by going though the usual red tape involved with such a situation.

I have been involved in many of these types of situations during the course of my career, and it's all worth the effort involved in order to broaden your horizons. Some institutions might require more paperwork and rigor than others, but the intent of all these processes is to protect the public and the facility, which is totally understandable.

It should be made clear at this point that these practice patterns are not the only options. Often there is a custom approach to the collaboration, and these are just examples of how things can be set up when starting a new office, or making that change. Also, this might seem like common sense to you, but with the excitement involved in situations like this, some basic principles relating to the locum tenens arrangement (e.g., conditions, financial arrangement) might be overshadowed by the moment.

5. FACTORS TO CONSIDER WHEN CHOOSING A STYLE OF PRACTICE

There are many things to consider when you are choosing the right style of practice for your needs. You need to consider the time commitments as well as the financial arrangements, options to continue, and possibilities for change.

5.1 Time commitment

Lifestyle is an important consideration for many. There is no question that certain health-care disciplines lend themselves to longer working hours than others. You do have some flexibility in what you choose, but as alluded to earlier in the book, there is no point in choosing something you are not going to enjoy.

A surgeon, for example, generally works longer hours than some other specialties, or than a primary care physician, the latter is usually more able to choose hours and working conditions. This, of course, depends on the work situation and desire of the individuals. A salaried health-care provider typically works within the confines of the employer. By the way, there are primary care physicians who work way harder than surgeons, by choice or by need.

It is up to you as to how much time you want to work in your new practice. Having said that, when you are starting out, you will likely have to spend long hours getting things off the ground, no matter what field. The situation in which you will have the most say over your time schedule is in a solo practice because you will not have to report to anyone, and you can determine your own schedule.

5.2 Financial arrangements

Financial arrangements depend on the type of office practice you choose. However, it does have to be emphasized that if you are in a solo

practice, you have way more independence regarding financial issues.

Whatever style of practice you choose, especially when you are not working for yourself, make sure you have full disclosure and the relevant documentation as to how you are going to be paid, and when. There is nothing worse than having to bicker over financial queries or misunderstandings once you have started. There is a fine balance as to how far you can go with clarifying these issues at the time of negotiation, but it is still better to do so before you have started, rather than after the fact.

5.3 Options for continuation

Whatever setup you choose, you have to look ahead and make sure of your abilities for continuation in the practice and if there are any warning signs to be aware of, such as a new establishment planned for the office location in five years. About the only safe option, which few health professionals find themselves in, is when you own the property and you are in a solo practice. All the other possibilities (i.e., associate, locum tenens, solo practice in a rented suite) need clarification in writing that you will not be kicked out after a certain time period.

Obviously, there are always unpredictable circumstances, such as a personality conflict, which will result in a premature change or end your association with a practice once a specified time period has elapsed. However, you should look at all options for continuation in a new office setup.

5.4 Possibility for change

Just as you ensure possibilities for continuation in a practice, you should also protect yourself by having an option for change at any time during your contract, or lease. While it will not be possible in many situations, you should at least try to look at options in the event of an unexpected change. The one that requires the least research in this regard is the solo practice in which you own the property yourself — all other practice arrangements can make for more challenging situations in the event of a proposed change.

Appropriate legal help should be sought before you commit to anything — it is worth every cent you invest at the outset.

5.5 Mobility

While mobility is often an attractive and positive thing, it can be a challenging situation too. Let me tell you how being mobile has given me an incredible experience and diversity in medicine and life. I did my undergraduate medical training and one-year internship in South Africa. I then ventured to Canada where I practiced for six months in the fishing outports of Newfoundland. From Newfoundland I moved out west to the province of Saskatchewan where I worked for four months as a general practitioner. By that time I decided I wanted to stay in Canada and had to do further medical training for a few months in areas that were not covered in my internship. After completing this training, I worked for almost three years as a family doctor in Saskatchewan. In the interim, I completed the Canadian licensing exams and became a permanent resident of Canada.

I then ventured to the University of Alberta in Edmonton for a residency-training program in Pediatrics, followed by an Otolaryngology training program at the University of Toronto, Ontario. I practiced for almost ten years in Toronto and then relocated to Vancouver, British Columbia.

During the years, I also completed the United States specialty certification exams and maintained my registration with the British Medical Council. All of this is mentioned for

one intention, and that is to show you how exciting some health professions can be in terms of mobility and opportunity for change

Mobility is not always that easy. While I have been able to do that which I just described, it does not mean I can automatically practice anywhere. Each country, state, and province has its own regulations. I, for one, would not be able to practice in certain states in the US without writing additional exams, and I would also need the appropriate work visa.

It depends where you originated from and where you did your training; there are some doctors and allied health professionals from certain parts of the world who could have problems trying to practice in another area. People from countries in which the language of training is not English, or in which the curriculum is entirely different, might have problems doing further training, or working, in an English-speaking country where things are quite different.

This works the same for English-speaking doctors who intend to move to a non-English speaking country. I know of many foreign-trained doctors in Canada, for example, who are unable to practice in this country. There are many complexities in this regard, including limited training positions, different backgrounds in terms of medical training, and possible language barriers. I am not sure if these physicians were fully aware of the limitations that faced them when trying to find a position as a physician (or even a retraining position) in their new home, but it must be very frustrating for these fully fledged doctors to not be able to do what they are trained to do.

This is an illustration of how mobility might not always work in your favor. Be sure to research all the details before embarking on a long career in medicine, or you might find you are sidelined by practice limitations purely based on a geographic location. One of the further challenges in this domain is also the fact that rules and regulations always change, and there is no guarantee that what was the case when you went into medicine will indeed be the same when you graduate.

Mobility can also be a factor when it comes to the type of discipline in which you choose to specialize. There are some areas in medicine in which moving from one geographical area to another is easier to do than others. A few examples of disciplines in which relocating is easier include anesthesiology, emergency medicine, intensive care, and pathology. Specialties that might be more challenging when moving are family medicine, pediatrics, surgery, and psychiatry. Typically the latter require you to set up an office and build a practice — closing shop and moving on is somewhat trickier. The former are included in the group that are either shift work, or specialties in which you are not responsible for a large number of patients that you take care of on an ongoing or long-term basis. Who would have thought that these things would come into play later when your training is complete and you are all setup, but its best to be informed of all the things that can happen when you are a health practitioner about to set up an office or even later when in practice.

Mobility is also similarly relevant to the other care professions. There are a multitude of options for working in another region or part of the world. Nurses, for example, often work in other countries for a prolonged period of time, with little roadblocks, other than obtaining a licence in a jurisdiction, or sometimes writing an extra exam. Often a location might be short of nurses, and will make the transition for nurses to work there as seamless as possible.

I am also aware of many of the other health-care fields, in which professionals have relocated far away and have had little difficulty setting up a practice, or career, in the new location. Just as easy as it is for some, other health-care providers might find it challenging, or almost impossible, to relocate. One example might be a naturopathic physician who in one country is permitted to function in similar ways to a physician with the ability to prescribe medication, while in another country might be limited as to practice options.

All these mobility issues are very variable and need to be individually researched when you are choosing a career and subsequently a place to practice. Either way, inquiring about your options once you are done your training as a health-care professional, is prudent and should be done earlier rather than later.

5.6 On-call

No matter what field you choose, or how mobile you are, at some point in your career or training you will have to be on-call. The nature and frequency of on-call can differ immensely from one health-care profession to the next. Almost all medical training programs require you to be on-call, albeit only during part of the program. The nature of on-call responsibilities and duties vary immensely. To follow are some examples of how being on-call can play out in the different stages of a career in medicine.

Being on-call in the office setting can pose challenges. You could be in the middle of a busy office, and get called away for an emergency, or have to deal with an emergency patient in the office. This has a significant impact on how the rest of the clinic, or day, will run, particularly if the emergency situation requires some time to sort out. This is the reality of many health-care professionals. Medical doctors, osteopathic physicians, dentists, veterinarians, and others could all be interrupted in the middle of a prescheduled day to take time out to deal with an acute on-call problem. This is not limited to primary health-care providers, generalists, or specialists — all fields have to deal with the reality of being on-call while in an office setting.

There are different strategies to deal with this problem. The first is to avoid choosing a discipline which lends to being on-call. This is possible in several fields, such as a developmental pediatrics, for nutritionists, or those in weight management.

For most health-care providers, this is not an option, as being on-call is part of the job. One option is not to book patients in the office when you are on-call, thus making yourself available for emergencies in the office, or another health-care facility, only. This is certainly a possibility, particularly if you work in a big urban area, and your situation allows you to do only occasional on-call duties. This is not an option if you work in another environment (e.g., there are only two general surgeons in the town in which you practice) and you are on-call a week at a time.

Whatever the situation, if you are on-call while seeing scheduled patients, it can be stressful on all parties involved — patients, staff, and yourself. You have to develop coping mechanisms so that everyone is on the same page. Patients need to be made aware of the fact that you might be called away by means of forms, signs, or some other method of communication. Your office staff should book your scheduling lightly for the day, to allow for any emergencies when on-call. You need to be up front with

patients and tell them what is going on — most people are understanding of such situations.

Having said all of this, there are some health-care professionals who choose to be on-call all the time, and having emergency patients, or situations, is a common occurrence. The one profession that comes to mind is dentistry — usually they will accommodate emergencies in between their regular patients, particularly if it is a problem involving one of their own patients.

While being on-call can be exciting and rewarding, many health-care professionals do not find this the most enjoyable part of the job. It all depends on the individual. Often being on-call can be quite stressful and thus some people dislike that part of their career. Others handle things better and are not really bothered by it at all.

You have to come to grips with the fact that if you want to pursue a career in a health-care profession, being on-call is likely going to be a big part of it. One senior mentor always told me that if there was one thing he could take out of his job, it would be the duty of being on-call. He then added that no job is perfect and he sees this duty as a necessity of being a doctor.

You have to take the good and bad and make the best of it; otherwise, you are going to be unhappy in what you do, which is no fun! What is more of an issue for you is if the bad is more than the good — it is then time to look at a career modification.

5.7 Flexibility

A career in medicine allows for amazing flexibility. This can be possible at so many different levels throughout the journey. It seems to me that the new generation of health-care workers value quality of life much more than their senior colleagues did in the past and do not shy away from taking time off work to have a more balanced life. More people are working part time, job sharing, and taking extended leaves of absence.

More women are going into medicine than in the past, and in several parts of the world — Canada being one example — the amount of women being admitted into medical schools at the present time exceeds the amount of men. With that comes more maternity leaves, but a health-care profession is often amenable to this type of flexibility. In recent years, paternity leave has also become more common. While it might be more difficult to take extended time off in some specialties than others, people seem to work well together to make these types of things happen. The fact that there are allowances now more so than ever for lifestyle choices means that some individuals are entering medical fields that might never before have considered this profession due to their personal situation.

It is also not uncommon for doctors to take a year, or longer, off from practice. This could be in the form of a sabbatical or other choice of activity — sometimes totally unrelated to medicine! This might be more difficult to do with some other professions but for many health-care professionals, especially academics and shift workers, it is certainly doable. This ease of movement and variety is yet another thing that people thinking about a career in medicine might not be fully aware of. Others only discover these types of opportunities after their office is up and running. While there are always options to make things happen if you want to take an extended leave, setting up your own office makes something like this a bit more challenging — something to keep in mind at the outset for those about to start a practice.

These are just a few examples of things that might not be on your radar screen when choosing a career, or setting up a practice. Much more will become evident as things progress in your career, as you are learning new and unique things. That's why it is always important to gain your wisdom from more than one source.

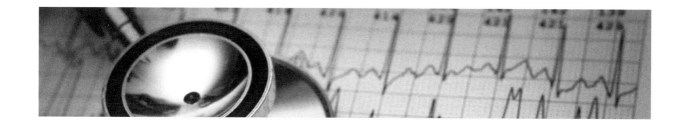

5

DEVELOP A BUSINESS PLAN
FOR YOUR PRACTICE

A business plan is a concept foreign to many health-care providers, and certainly was not part of my plan with my office setups. While much of what I did with checklists and priorities was almost like a business plan, it lacked some of the basics that should be considered when opening any new business.

The business plan discussed in this chapter is what I feel is pertinent to a medical doctor or any other health-care professional opening an office and might not apply to other enterprises. It should be mentioned that while the emphasis relating to a new medical office setup is health-care oriented and patient focused, it is still a business and you will need to keep that in mind every step of the way.

1. THE BUSINESS PLAN

The business plan is primarily needed to organize ideas in one place, both for quick reference and monitoring of progress. This can be used in conjunction with checklists and other documentation. It helps to keep you focused on the tasks relating to goals and the end point. It should be constructed with realistic expectations, but may have to be adjusted along the way. As with the checklists included in the book and on the CD, it gives you the opportunity to write something down on paper (or electronically!), which is your first step to getting the job done effectively and on time. Note that the CD includes an outline of a business plan to help you get started in creating your own plan.

Many new business owners will need help with financing from an institution when they are first setting up practice, after lengthy training and the associated debts. Some, even after years of practice, will need financial help when setting up a new office. A business plan will usually be needed by a bank, other financial institution, or investors to convince them to loan you the money. The type of profession and earning potential will often not be sufficient for someone to help you with a loan when you are just starting out. A realistic business plan shows others that you are serious and will be able to create a profitable business.

1.1 Executive summary

An executive summary is basically an introduction to the business plan. Usually this summary is an overview of what will be discussed in the entire business plan. No matter what task you are doing, I have always found an executive summary to be a challenging yet necessary undertaking. It forces you to think logically, prioritize what you want to say, and include the most important facts, ideas, and concepts within a limited space.

This summary is usually the section that is the most important information for the interested party, whether it is a bank, landlord, city official, or business partner. Of all the sections of the business plan, this is the one that is likely to be read most thoroughly. The reader will also see if you are focused on your goals and able to think logically at the outset of the business plan.

Note that the executive summary is located at the beginning of the document, but it is often the last part written because it is a summary of everything in your business plan.

1.2 The mission statement

The mission statement explains in one or two sentences what the business is trying to accomplish. The following examples will give you an idea of what a mission statement is:

Mission statement for a new family medicine office

To provide the best possible medical care to our patients of all ages and backgrounds. With the help of an efficient, collaborative office approach, we will provide a safe, caring, and supportive environment for patient care.

Mission statement for a new pediatric dentistry practice

Our dental office strives to provide exemplary dental care for children of all ages and walks of life. Our team approach of qualified and caring staff will make the dental experience for children and their caregivers as seamless as possible.

1.3 History and background

The history and background section of the business plan is where you are able to showcase all your training, experience, awards, research, publications, presentations, and so forth. This is basically a summary of your curriculum vitae, outlining your skills and strengths. It should also reflect on your dedication and ambition to show the other party that you have what it takes to open a business in your field. As an appendix to this section, you might consider including your full curriculum vitae for review.

The following list includes the type of things that should be in the description of your practice:

- Name of the practice
- Type of practice
- Scope of the practice
- Location of the practice
- Licenses necessary to open a practice

- Certifications that are beneficial for a practice of this nature

- Regulations that have to be abided by

- Office accreditation procedures

1.4 Practice values

The practice values section of the business plan discusses the values that should serve as a guide for practice conduct. Values should be defined to represent the practice, specialty, and profession. This is a particularly important section in which trust can be gained by someone who is considering joining your practice, loaning money to you, or investing in your establishment. These values should be an integral part of your practice, and exemplified by all employees, and this point should be made well known in this section.

Include some examples and situations that show the readers the following points:

- Pride, honesty, and transparency

- Nondiscriminatory practice policies

- Principles with patient treatment (e.g., age limits, when not to accept patients)

- Understanding of a diverse patient population in your area

- Treatment of patients with no health insurance or money to pay for services

- Coverage after hours

- Acceptable wait times

1.5 Operations and employees

The operations and employees section is an opportunity to discuss the organizational management and employee structure of the practice. The type of information to include in this section:

- How many employees will work at the practice.

- What type of employees (e.g., full time, part time)

- Contractual arrangements

You may also want to include a list of proposed staff at the time of setup and projected changes in the future. The following two are examples of what you may want to include in this section of your business plan:

Example 1

Staff at time of setup:

Dermatologists: 2

Nurses: 1

Medical office assistants: 3

External dictation service: Contractual basis

Predicted staff in three years:

Dermatologists: 3

Nurses: 1

Medical office assistants: 3

Example 2

Staff at time of setup:

Physiotherapists: 2

Occupational therapist: 1

Medical office assistant: 1

Predicted staff in two years:

Physiotherapists: 3

Occupational therapist: 1

Massage therapist: 1

Medical office assistants: 2

Bookkeeper: 1

1.6 Market research

You want to make sure that whoever is reading the business plan believes that you have done your homework before setting up an expensive new office. As mentioned in several areas of this book, research is the key to success no matter what stage you are at in your health-care field.

Specifically important concepts to convey in this section include:

- Demand versus supply. Will there be sufficient patient volume for your practice?

- Provide a number of similar health-care providers in the area and, if you can, a provider-to-population ratio.

- Do you have a skill set that is unique to the area? Can you offer a service that is not provided in the area, or is in high demand? If so, describe your situation.

- Do you have some type of evidence to show that a professional like yourself is needed in the catchment area?

1.7 Marketing strategy

In the marketing strategy area you can highlight the methods you intend to use to promote yourself, and your practice. While marketing aspects for a new practice are covered in Chapter 11 in more detail, the type of information to include in your business plan is how you plan to market your practice. In other words, how you plan to get the word out so that you will have patients when you open the doors to your new business.

You may want to discuss how you will distribute an introductory letter to the relevant health-care providers and institutions in the area to get the word out that you are open for business. You may also want to include information about your distribution of announcement cards or mass mailings through email.

If you are going to advertise using print ads or TV commercials, describe advertisements and how they will reach your intended target market. Your marketing strategy may be more low-key and less expensive, such as going out into the community and talking to other health-care professionals and practices in the area and leaving behind business cards.

1.8 Financial plan

The financial plan is a critical part of the business plan, especially if funding is needed from a bank or elsewhere to help you set up your office. It is important to take the most time writing this part of your business plan, especially if you need funding. The following information needs to be covered in this section of your business plan:

- Proposed plans for start-up costs

- How billing is going to take place

- When the practice is going to start making a profit

- Prediction of how long it will take to recoup start-up costs

You may want to hire a financial planner, consultant, or accountant to help you figure out the details of your financial plan. If you are going to hire a financial professional on a contract or permanent basis after your business is up and running, you may also want to include that information in your financial plan so that the intended reader knows you are serious about the financial setup and future of the business.

1.9 Forecasts and predictions

You can make forecasts for the future in this section, but you also need to give careful thought as to what might happen if things don't go as planned. Like any business, many aspects of health care can change with time, affecting your practice in ways that are unpredictable. It is important that you think carefully about your ideals and expectations in a realistic way.

The forecasts and predictions section will help you envision where you want your company to be in the next three to five years. Do you want to expand and have other professionals sharing your office (e.g., a chiropractor hiring a massage therapist to also practice in the same office)? Will you expand your practice to include additional equipment and services?

Basically this section covers realistic goals that you want to strive for in the coming years.

2. REVISITING YOUR BUSINESS PLAN

Your business plan should always be reviewed and revisited after a stipulated period of time. You might decide that after two years, for example, it would be a good time to look at your situation and business plan again.

Being comprehensive, realistic, insightful and, in the future, reflective, can only help the overall impression of your business plan, your character, and the future nature of the practice.

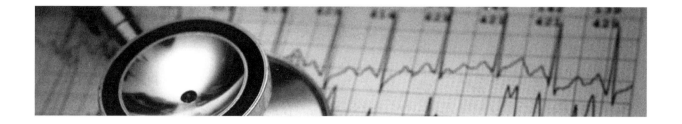

6

DECIDING ON A FACILITY AND LOCATION FOR YOUR OFFICE

There are several factors that can come into play when you are deciding where to set up your practice. Things to consider include a desirable location for you, the size of the office building, what services are available in the building, and what facilities or services are in the near vicinity. This chapter will discuss all these things, and more, that need to be taken into account when choosing a location.

1. PROXIMITY TO ANCILLARY SERVICES

An important decision at the outset is where you want your practice to be located. In smaller communities you often do not have a choice, but in bigger cities there can be a multitude of options. One of the major factors is what type of health-care provider you are, and whether

you need to be close to medical facilities or not. The following are a few examples to illustrate this point.

Dr. Frank is a psychiatrist who has a practice with an interest in psychotherapy. He does not work in the emergency room and does not have a need for inpatients. Also, he has chosen not to be on staff at the local community hospital. Because he doesn't frequently need to request investigations (e.g., blood work and X-rays) for his patients, there is no need for a laboratory to be close to his office. Based on the needs of his patients, he has more flexibility as to where the office can be physically located. Dr. Frank has chosen to work in a rented part of a commercial house; the other tenants in the house being a small legal firm. Dr. Frank's office is on the second floor, with shared basement storage facilities for both practices. This office is located in a residential area and parking is abundant and without cost.

Dr. Vans is a newly qualified general surgeon who has managed to secure a teaching position in the hospital in the downtown core — something not always easy to do when first starting out in practice. As she will frequently require laboratory and radiology services for her patients, she needs to be in a facility where patients can readily obtain the necessary type of investigations, both conveniently and expediently. Dr. Vans has chosen the professional building across the street from the hospital where she does her surgeries and on-call work.

While the ancillary services are somewhat limited in the professional building, Dr. Vans' office is opposite the teaching hospital that is right across the street. She can get the basic tests ordered and processed in the professional building where her office is located. For the more complex investigations, they do not have to go far; everything is available close by. The parking, however, is limited in the area and is ridiculously expensive.

Dr. Smith is an infectious disease specialist who is deciding on where to set up his consulting office. Besides working in the wards and emergency department most of the time, his outpatients also require frequent investigations, many of which can only be processed in the hospital setting due to the complexity of the problems and subsequent advanced investigations required. For that reason, Dr. Smith has opted to use some space in the hospital for his outpatient work — an area dedicated for ambulatory care. The rent is slightly less expensive than if he would be renting outside the hospital, and he was able to negotiate on the percentage of expenses he is required to pay relating to some of the shared services and support staff, thus making this a very viable plan.

2. GROUP ENVIRONMENT VERSUS STAND ALONE

We all have our own preferences as to how we best function, and wish to practice. Some people like being on their own, in a solo practice, while others prefer a group environment. As alluded to briefly in Chapter 4, I have worked in both those situations and I must say each has their benefits and drawbacks. The specialty you are in will also dictate whether you will be able to work on your own or not.

On the one hand, an intensive-care specialist will have to work in a unit located in a hospital, or similar appropriate health-care setting. The specialist's office will have to be close to the intensive care, so that if he or she is needed fast, the trip is brief. The optimum running of an intensive care unit is a team effort involving different health-care disciplines, and being just down the hall from these people will make things that much easier. A family physician, on the other hand, who has decided to specialize in nutrition and diet management, can work entirely on his or her own away from other health-care professionals or facilities, if he or she so chooses. These are just a couple of examples where there might be different levels of flexibility depending on which field is practiced.

Besides working in an office where you are sharing with other medical doctors, there are many different options for you as to who you wish to have working with you under the same roof, or at least hope for. You can choose to work only with medical doctors, or you can be part of a multidisciplinary team. There are many physicians who choose to share the same office space and overhead with other health-care professionals. There are practical and financial benefits to such a setup. I have seen, and experienced, many such shared offices, including medical doctors paired up with chiropractors, nurse practitioners, audiologists, speech-language pathologists, podiatrists, and many similar situations. The convenience for your patients who might need the multidisciplinary approach for their optimal health care is self-evident.

3. BUILDING FACILITIES

Medical services, within a professional building, geared toward the health-care professions can vary enormously. There are some medical buildings that just offer the bare minimum in terms of ancillary services, examples being a laboratory or basic radiology provider (e.g., X-rays and ultrasounds). Other buildings can be loaded with a whole gamut of testing and other services such as a CT scanner, MRI imaging, nuclear scanning, and audiology, just to name a few.

Another important factor is whether retail options are in the same building as your office, or at least in close proximity. For some health-care providers, this service might be a deal breaker. Examples of such enterprises could include a pharmacy, medical home-care product store, orthoptics (e.g., limb prostheses), and optician — the need for these services and conveniences at your doorstep all depend on what type of practice you have.

I have also seen arrangements in which doctors share space with retail businesses such as pharmacies. The acceptance of this philosophy of practice, or business negotiation, varies enormously, some licensing bodies discouraging or disallowing this type of association. There is always the possibility of conflict of interest with a situation like this — a doctor potentially prescribing more medications than might be needed, obviously benefiting the pharmacy. On the flip side, the pharmacy might be renting the space for a reduced amount, hoping for lots of prescriptions; the income from this prescribing practice in excess

of what could be obtained from an increased rental arrangement. I would hope this type of association is not common, and I believe these things are usually figured out one way or another with potential detrimental consequences for the physician, and others involved.

While many health-care professionals have a preference for medical-type buildings and environments, there are others who prefer working in a more commercial setting. Many large malls have dentist offices. Having the foot traffic go by on a daily basis will undoubtedly increase the new patient load. Also, for the multitude of employees in the mall, some will enjoy the convenience associated with having a dentist close to their work. This alleviates transportation and/or parking costs. I would imagine the rents are very high in malls, likely creating a higher cost for the patients. I have also seen medical offices and other allied health professions in malls, both indoor and strip malls.

Having a snack bar or restaurant in the building can be very helpful. This can help you and your staff, particularly during short lunch breaks, and your patients who have to arrive early or wait lengthy periods before been seen.

4. ACCESS FOR THE DISABLED

Adequate access for disabled patients who visit your office should be standard practice. This is something that has been neglected in years gone by. Nowadays, many jurisdictions in the world have stringent rules and regulations with regard to mandatory provisions for the disabled in the office setting.

While this might be less of a problem in a medical building that already has the necessary provisions in place, this is important to have on your checklist if you have to design, or redo, your own office space within a professional building, or more importantly have your own, small, stand-alone facility. During the planning stage, always keep in mind details such as corridors, angles, and door widths in your design. The building experts are well informed of these details, but may not be familiar with how things might function in your specific situation or practice.

In the office that I developed with help from a designer, I did take accessibility into account, but I still remember some tight wheelchair manoeuvering by patients at times. This resulted in some minor bumps and scratches on the wall, and the periodic need for me to touch up the paint. In retrospect, we could have made the corridors just a little wider and the angles less acute. So, keep disability considerations at the forefront, and do not always take other people's expertise as a given. Try to figure things out for your unique situation, together with experts.

Necessary accommodations for the disabled are also of paramount importance when looking at the actual building you choose. Are there adequate parking spots for disabled people? Are there appropriate ramps present for wheelchair access? How about push button opportunities for entrances and exits? Are the public washrooms adequately fitted for special needs? Are the elevators equipped for your hearing and vision-challenged patients? While many of these questions might seem simple at the outset, it is better to have them on the radar screen when considering a location for your practice, rather than discovering these things after the fact.

5. WASHROOMS

I have worked in so many different environments where washroom facilities are in different areas — in the office itself, in the communal corridor outside the office, or even on a different floor. If you have any say in the matter, or you have the ability to be involved in the initial plans, try your best to negotiate for a washroom in your own office space. Even if it is small and only available for staff use, this will be a huge convenience for you.

I have worked in several offices, when in the middle of a busy clinic, I have to take a key for the washroom, walk through the patient waiting area, come back through the patient waiting area, and then return to seeing the patients. I have always appreciated having the convenience of a washroom in the office itself as opposed to the inconvenience of an external trek to find one. This is one of those things that may not be on your mind with your initial considerations of the place, but try your best to have a washroom in your own space if you have the choice.

Easily accessible public washrooms are also important for your patients. Besides the obvious need for your patients to have access to a toilet, frequently doctors' offices require specimens such as urine samples, which have to be obtained there and then. The toilet might be less than adequate for these types of needs, and if you don't think of this in the beginning, it's more difficult to modify things after you have moved in and everything is in place.

Some medical offices have unique arrangements in the washroom for processing urine specimens. I have seen toilets that have shelves designed specifically for holding urine specimens; other restrooms might have a small door in the wall with a shelf, which allow the patients to place the specimen cups in it and a lab technician to take them from the other side of the wall when the patients leave the restroom. These small things can simplify the process, and make the ordeal that much easier and less intrusive for your patients and more convenient for your staff.

While in section **4.** I already mentioned disability considerations, it can never be stressed enough to keep this in mind when looking at toilet options, and related design. While most medical offices have adequate provisions in place already, others do not, and your diligence in being thorough with plans is essential.

6. PUBLIC TRANSPORT AND PARKING

Depending on the environment you choose to work in, and your health-care discipline, close access to public transport and parking can sometimes be a deal breaker for your patients. Many people will choose a health-care provider based on convenience and ease when it comes to making a visit. Having sufficient parking on the premises, or reasonable parking within the close vicinity is really important to some people. For others, the cost of the parking could be a strong consideration. There are more questions for you to consider when looking at parking, keeping patient and staff safety in mind. Is the parking lot well-lit at night? Is there security in the area? Is the parking in a secured parking lot with security guards?

Some patients might not even consider parking a factor and prefer a medical practice that is in closer proximity to public transportation. Of equal, if not more importance, and in keeping with environmental and sustainability responsibilities, public transport might be the preferred choice for many. Also, riding a bicycle is becoming more and more popular, when ability, distance, location, and weather allow for this. On that note, making sure there is a bicycle rack should be another thing for you to check. This being a health-related book, I do have to mention the obvious health benefits of riding a bike or walking!

I recall a parking dilemma when I was in a medium-sized office building in a large metropolitan area. There were almost equally sized office buildings across the road from each other; the road was a major traffic thoroughfare with little street parking. Both these buildings had free parking, one with ample spots always available, the other parking lot consistently full with cars often circling around looking for parking. I frequently heard patients' elevator conversations about choosing doctors, and related services, based on the parking situation. Some patients even parked at the professional building that usually had more spots available and then walked across the road to the other facility where parking was tight; when these situations came to light many people were not happy about it.

Always keep transportation and parking options on the radar screen when choosing your new office. This certainly is a big factor if your patients have choices when picking a health-care provider. When you have things all sorted out in your office, do your patients a big favor: Have a one-page handout for them with all relevant transportation information such as parking options and costs, details about public transport, and availability of bicycle racks. These little things will go a long way toward patient satisfaction and an overall good experience in your new office.

Checklist 1 will help you decide on an appropriate facility for your office. The CD includes a printable version of this checklist. Print a few copies and take them with you when you look at potential offices. Write the facility address at the top of the checklist and then use the checkboxes to check what the office has to fit your needs. You may also want to make notes below the topics to review later.

CHECKLIST 1
DECIDING ON A FACILITY FOR YOUR OFFICE

Facility address: _____

Proximity to Ancillary Services

Is your practice close to the following services?

☐ Laboratory

☐ Radiology (X-rays, etc.)

☐ Hospital-based services

☐ Other: _____

☐ Other: _____

☐ Other: _____

Building Services

If you have chosen a building with other services, does it include what you need?

☐ Laboratory

☐ Radiology (X-rays, etc.)

☐ Pharmacy

☐ Home-care equipment

☐ Other retail enterprise of need to patients (e.g., optician)

☐ Food on premises or close by

☐ Other: _____

☐ Other: _____

Access for the Disabled

☐ Is the facility user-friendly for your disabled patients?

☐ Have you reviewed standard provisions within the building?

☐ Look at specifics in your potential office; is it easily accessible?

☐ Is there enough room for wheelchairs to get through doors, corridors, and around corners?

☐ Are there appropriate ramps present for wheelchair access?

☐ Are there push buttons for automatic door entrances and exits?

☐ Are the public washrooms adequately fitted for special needs?

☐ Are the elevators equipped with features for the visually and hearing impaired?

☐ Other: _____

☐ Other: _____

Washrooms

☐ Is the washroom located in the office?

☐ Is the washroom in a convenient location for patients?

☐ Is there easy access for your staff to obtain the urine samples provided by patients?

☐ Is there an appropriate holding area for specimens?

☐ Other: _____

Public Transport and Parking

☐ Have you reviewed parking availability?

☐ Is there a nearby public transport stop and route?

☐ Have you considered the costs of both public transport and parking for your patients?

☐ Have you examined street parking in the area and the potential limitations?

☐ Are there adequate handicap parking spots?

☐ Is the parking lot well-lit at night?

☐ Is there security in the area? Or is there a need for security in that neighborhood?

☐ Is the parking in a secured parking lot with security?

☐ Will you need to create a handout so patients understand transport information?

☐ Are there bicycle racks in the area or close to the building?

☐ Other: _____

7. OTHER FACTORS TO CONSIDER WHEN CHOOSING YOUR OFFICE

When you have chosen a location, your next step is to consider the places that you are viewing and how they will fit your office needs. You want to make sure you have enough square footage for your office and that the design of the office is what you want, or if not, that you will be able to alter it to fit your needs. Other considerations include security for your staff and patients, privacy for patients, and storage.

7.1 Square footage

While it is always good to have ample space, in most situations you will be responsible for paying for every square meter, or foot, of space. Often you will not have a choice as to the square footage because the office is already built and designed with little room for modification, if any. In other situations, you will be able to plan the office space from scratch and choose exactly what you want.

In my experience, where an office setup was already in place, I was able to negotiate the lease payments.

If possible, reducing your office space is one way you can reduce costs. In my situation of being able to choose space from a bare floor plan, I worked with the landlord, and the designer, to create a brand new space relevant to my needs. I remember shaving off some square footage wherever I could to reduce the price. More space meant more money to pay, and as a young surgeon I wanted to keep the overhead and expenses as low as possible keeping in mind all the debts that are incurred with a new office setup.

7.2 Design of the office

I can remember so many things that were taken into account when considering the plans for the design of my solo office. Of utmost importance to me were functionality and convenience of patient flow.

Choose your layout wisely. Things will run so much more smoothly if attention to detail is paid during the planning stages of your new office. How far do your patients have to walk from the waiting room to the examining room? Can the patients see or hear what's going on in another examination area? It is important to be cognizant of confidentiality every step of the way in your planning stages. Try and visualize incoming and exiting patients, and how much space they have to move around, so people are not bumping into each other!

7.3 Adequate examination rooms

Are the examination rooms big enough for everything that needs to be in the room? Every type of health-care professional, depending on their specialty, will require their own unique layout, some requiring much more equipment and working space than others. Some examination rooms will require drawers, closet or storage space, examination beds, examination chairs, or desks in the room itself, while others might only need the bare minimum.

Know exactly what you need when planning, and use a measuring tape for everything. Do not try and guess how everything is going to fit! Make sure you map out the exact layout of how you envision the room, and do not take any shortcuts in the planning phase. If you need some help from a professional who has experience with this, do not hesitate to ask for help. Be sure to draw a diagram for the planned layout — visualizing in your mind is not enough!

One factor that is always a question for health-care providers is whether to have a washing sink in all the examination rooms.

This is no doubt dependent on the health-care field you are in. This can mean fairly major modifications for your design plans as well as significant extra expense in the renovations. The liberal and effective use of hand sanitizers has also changed the absolute need to have washing sinks in all exam rooms. This is something you will have to decide depending on your unique situation, but do not forget to include sinks in your overall plans.

Being stuck in a setup that is below your needs is often not worth the other benefits that might be present when choosing this area of space for your practice. I recall deciding against several potential office space options, and better financial deals, for the sole reason that exam rooms were too small, or there were inadequate working spaces for my type of practice.

7.4 Adequate patient waiting area

It is not a good situation to have patients standing and waiting to be seen, with all the available seats being taken up. The demands of waiting area space is very much dependent on the type of practice you are in. If you have a low-volume practice with one patient being seen every hour, then you need just a few seats present in your waiting room. If you have a high-volume practice, with several patients going through your office in a short period of time, it's important to have lots of space available.

This might be an easier thing to sort out if you have a choice about the design of your waiting room at the outset. You can thus plan accordingly with sufficient sitting space. If you move into a space where the area is too small, you might have to change things around in your waiting room to make more sitting space for your patients. It is in this very specific situation that someone, or a company, with expertise in this type of design could help you enormously with the design of the waiting area.

7.5 Noise considerations

Every practice has different needs when it comes to noise considerations. There are certain clinical domains where noise distractions are important to avoid. Take, for example, an audiologist's practice; or an ear, nose, and throat specialist who performs hearing testing. You can only imagine what type of distractions could result from background noise during testing that requires silence. While most of this type of testing is done in a soundproof booth, unnecessary noise can be detrimental to the accuracy of the results.

Another example could be a psychotherapist, or someone who utilizes hypnosis as a mode of treatment. Having all kinds of noise, of any origin, including street noises, will not blend in well with a practice of this nature. Noise is not a common factor that you might take into consideration when first looking at a new office, but if this is not carefully considered, it can become quite a distraction once you have moved in.

One of the things that I did not realize when I designed my first office from bare floor plans was how conversations can carry from one area to the next, particularly relating to patient encounters. With the initial plan, I thought it would be a great idea to have an open-concept arrangement for the reception area. With this setup, there were many waiting room chairs in close vicinity to the reception desk and hallway. I liked this because there was lots of open space and light that filtered to the patient waiting area. It soon became apparent that whenever the office assistant was on the phone dealing with sensitive information, half the patients in the waiting room could hear what was going on. It did not take long before we added on a partition to the reception desk area, separating the office staff from the waiting area. This included a sliding window that the secretary could open and close as needed. While this seemed less friendly and uninviting, protecting patient confidentiality was crucial. This also lessened distractions for the front staff who had lots on the go. It didn't take my staff and I long to get used to the new, more "closed off" environment.

Having appropriate barriers between examination rooms and waiting areas is, needless to say, an important issue to keep in mind. Your patients will really appreciate being in a safe milieu to say what's on their mind and not worry about who is listening in. You also need to be able to have a private setting for your more sensitive conversations with patients.

7.6 Storage space

Storage space is also something that is commonly overlooked when choosing an office space. Certain health-care professionals require more storage space than others. Some storage space should preferably be within the office, and not in another area such as in a basement. Another option is off-site storage for files, but you need to have some system in place for keeping the more urgent, or recent, documents closer at hand.

Something people tend to forget is that unless a premise is a "paper-free office" (i.e., electronic-based office) files build up fast and you need space for them. I frequently had to make plans to have older files moved off-site to make way for new ones. I also had to redesign the existing storage space to allow for more efficient use of space and new files.

Further advice concerning file management will be mentioned later when it comes to retention of files (see Chapter 13). Whatever your eventual storage needs are, always keep it on your checklist for consideration when choosing a location for your practice. There are companies that specialize in effective storage

so research to find out what company will suit your needs.

7.7 Dedicated child play area

Depending on the practice, and the ages of your patient population, one of the things you might consider is a separate play area for your pediatric patients. This may not be possible depending on the circumstances of your new office, limitation of space, or design.

I have always worked in an environment in which lots of children are part of my patient mix. I have found the best setup is to have a designated area as a children's play area. It can be walled off with a low partition to allow the children to remain in a confined area, together with all the toys you have available for them. Such an area has to be completely childproof with regard to potential injuries. I had the low walls covered with a soft carpet fabric as well as modified corners to help prevent any injuries. Making these things as childproof as possible at the outset is prudent and essential. You do not want these modifications to only come into effect when adverse situations arise; that's why it is imperative to be proactive with childproofing such an area. You also need to be able to seat parents close by, so they can watch their children in the play area. For more on child safety, see Chapter 13.

By having a separate section, you can keep all the toys and books in one area away from the rest of your waiting room (it won't look like a tornado has hit it, with children's toys scattered throughout your office). In addition, it will attempt to keep the children in a confined space, instead of having them running around the office. While this separate area is a good idea, it does not always do the trick, and you could still have your young patients doing exactly what they want to do despite your best intentions!

This type of layout is particularly important when you have an office of mixed patients, namely adults, children, professionals, and others — adults like to feel welcome as well!

7.8 Security

Security is dependent on many factors, including location of practice, type of practice, and other considerations that you might not be aware of until you move into the office. There can be different levels of security in any one setting and different people who are responsible for them. There is the possibility of security that is the responsibility of the building or facility. This type of security you might have little control over. There might also be an opportunity for security in your unit, thus giving you more latitude as to what system you install.

If there is inadequate building security, an in-office alarm system should be considered. Remember there is no point in getting an alarm system without the appropriate "alert and respond" system. You need provisions in place in case an alarm goes off — there are so many different companies who take care of these type of things, so do your research.

Besides the obvious materialistic loss with a burglary, there are medications that can get in the wrong hands and sensitive personal patient information that can be breached, which includes what's on your computers and in your files. It is your responsibility to ensure that patient records are safe, and if an alarm system is needed, so be it.

7.9 Side entrance

A side entrance is a very handy extra convenience. Sometimes you have to urgently leave the office in the middle of a clinic to rush to the hospital for whatever reason. Other times you might arrive late for your office start time due to an emergency at the hospital. It is always easier to deal with these situations if you have a separate entrance that you can utilize. Not only will it be easier for you, but you will avoid patients awaiting your arrival or observing your every move.

While this is something neat to have in order to "escape" or for a justifiable late arrival, it is not meant in any way to mislead your patients. It is the responsibility of your office staff to appropriately inform your patients if unexpected situations arise where their appointment time may be delayed or cancelled. Nobody likes to wait a long time in the waiting room whatever the reason is. Skilled and experienced office staff can alleviate much of the problems that can arise in a situation like this with adequate communication.

7.10 Signage

Signage is one of the things that often gets overlooked, or forgotten. When setting up a practice make sure your signage is arranged for far enough in advance. Having signs made for you can take more time than you might think. I have experienced a longer than envisioned wait for a sign to be designed and installed — in my situation this process took months. This situation resulted in a handwritten sign being created and it was present for quite a while before the permanent one arrived. Be sure to do this very early in your set-up process.

Also, carefully review your planned signage, or the proofs, beforehand. Most professionals in this business will provide you with a copy, or draft, for you to review for final approval. Also, be very diligent with the spelling and titles when reviewing the information. It will be expensive for you if the sign has to be redone. Usually this is all very automatic if you are dealing with the right people, but if not, the onus is on you to get things right.

I can recall at least one situation, despite due diligence, where the final product was not entirely what I wanted and had to be redone. It was a long wait for the redesigned sign and it was expensive.

Checklist 2 will help you keep organized when considering other factors for choosing an office. The CD includes a printable version of this checklist. Just as you did with Checklist 1, write the facility address at the top of the checklist and then use the checkboxes to check what the office has to fit your needs. You may also want to make notes below the topics to review later.

8. PURCHASE VERSUS RENTAL

From my experience, the majority of doctors and health-care professionals do not own their practice premises, but instead rent or lease. You will need to decide the best situation for you. The following sections will discuss both the purchase and rental options.

8.1 Purchasing a house or condo for an office

If you are a newly graduated health-care professional, you might not be in a position to purchase a property for use as your office when you are just starting out. However, I do know of at least one colleague who did buy a house early on in his career that he now uses as his medical office. Something like this might make financial sense in a specific situation. There are many advantages to practicing in a place that you own, particularly if you plan major renovations or even minor design — the money you spend on improvements belongs to you, versus renovating someone else's property. With the design, you can choose what you want, and to your personal taste. If you rent, you are often limited with what you can do, and the changes have to be approved by the landlord. Also,

purchasing can be a wise investment for you, depending on the present real estate market.

Buying an office in a professional building is very much like buying a unit in a condominium complex. There will be taxes, maintenance fees, and all the other costs involved with owning your own condo. As is the case with any of these building situations, you could be faced with special assessments and costs involved with major repairs or upgrades.

It is actually not uncommon for people who are practicing in remote areas, where professional facilities and appropriate office space are not readily available, to set up a medical office as part of their residence. The purchase of property for this dual purpose could have several benefits. Besides the unbelievable convenience of having the office in your home, there can be added financial benefits, such as business tax deductions. Other benefits include the ease of having your own kitchen where breaks for coffee or lunch can be taken, and the time saved by being just a few steps away from your workplace.

One of the disadvantages of having your practice in your home is that patients know where to find you at all times, and you will never truly be "off duty." While patients usually respect the privacy of a health-care professional in a situation like this, it would be hard for any person to ignore banging in the middle of the night on his or her front door regarding some type of medical emergency needing attention. Another disadvantage is that you are so close to home, you might have difficulty with work boundaries and find yourself stuck doing paperwork after the work day is done, when ordinarily you would have left the office for the day. You would no doubt also have to be good at separating barriers from your home setting so that none of your family walk into the middle of a patient consultation, or visit your patients in the waiting room.

CHECKLIST 2
OTHER FACTORS TO CONSIDER WHEN CHOOSING AN OFFICE

Facility address: _____

Square Footage

☐ Is the space adequate for your needs?

☐ Can you reduce square footage to save money?

☐ If it is more space than you need, can you negotiate the price?

Design of Office Layout

☐ Is the layout functional and convenient for patient flow?

☐ Will the patients have a long way to walk from the waiting room to the examining room?

☐ Does the design provide confidentiality and noise barriers?

☐ Do you need to consider professional help with the design?

☐ Have you used a measuring tape to help with your planning of the layout?

Adequate Examination Rooms

☐ Are the exam rooms an appropriate size?

☐ Is the layout of the exam rooms functional for your practice?

☐ Can the patients see or hear what's going on in another examination area?

☐ Are the examination rooms big enough for everything that needs to be in the rooms?

☐ Are there washing sinks in the exam rooms?

☐ Do you need to install washing sinks?

Adequate Patient Waiting Area

☐ Is the patient waiting area the appropriate size for your practice?

☐ Will the waiting area have sufficient space for the number of seats necessary for patients?

☐ If it is a small area, can you be innovative with seating design?

☐ Do you need to hire professional help with the layout of the waiting area?

Noise Considerations

☐ Does the layout suit your practice for noise considerations?

☐ Is there street noise or other noise pollution that will affect your practice?

☐ Is there privacy for your front staff to conduct their jobs?

☐ Are there adequate barriers between examination rooms and the waiting area?

Storage Space

☐   Is there enough storage space onsite?

☐   Is the location of storage space adequate?

☐   Is the storage space located in a separate area of the building?

☐   Will you have to rent storage space outside the office premises?

Dedicated Child Play Area

☐   Will you have lots of children visiting your practice?

☐   Is there enough room to provide a child play area?

☐   What are some of your ideas about childproofing an area?

Security

☐   Is there building and facility security?

☐   Is there internal office security?

☐   Is the security system effective?

☐   Is there an appropriate security response system?

☐   Do you need to get expert help with security?

Side Entrance

☐   Is there a private side entrance?

Signage

☐   Have you ordered your business sign?

☐   Have you reviewed the proofs?

☐   What is the time line to get the finished sign and will it be hung before you open your practice?

8.2 Renting office facilities

None of us like to pay more money than is required for anything in life, and paying rent for your office is no different. While a specific office might seem the ideal setup for you at first glance, do your homework with regard to how much you should be paying. Shop around in the area and look at what else is available. Get competitive rates for the area you are interested in opening your practice and have a good sense of what the going rate per square foot is in the area.

Also, be very cognizant of what the availability and demand is like in the geographic area in which you are looking. If there are lots of places available in the area, this may be a powerful bargaining tool for you. If the area is in high demand, and there are not a lot of places available, it might alert you to the fact that you have little room for negotiations. It's always best to try to negotiate for the best possible rent, and if you don't explore the possibility of a "better deal," you will never know otherwise.

Sometimes even a bit of compromise on another aspect of your lease, or contract, might be a viable alternative. Reserved parking spots included in the lease is one example in which you can negotiate — that is, if you do not need all the allocated spots. Forfeiting some space (e.g., storage area), is another example in which you might have room to negotiate on your lease arrangement. Just remember there are real estate agents who do specialize in rental or lease arrangements — consider their services if you feel ill equipped to deal with this yourself.

8.3 Lease considerations

One thing most of us do not usually learn much about in medical school is the business side of the medical practice, but this is somewhat variable from one school to the next. Signing a lease is one example of an area I knew little about,

particularly in the professional setting. It was quite the educational experience, something I wish I had known more about beforehand.

My best advice is for you to read the small print carefully on any lease agreement you are considering signing. You need to be aware of all the details before signing on the dotted line. Do not be naive, and don't think this is like those contracts you readily accept on the Internet when downloading music or a movie. There can be significant long-term ramifications for you, if you do not carefully scrutinize the lease.

It is very exciting getting your first practice, but you need to be cognizant of the limitations, and consequences, that can affect you committing yourself in signing a lease. The lease is a binding document, often with little flexibility or ability to change. Just remember, these contractual obligations are set up in the best interests of the landlord and not yourself. You have to think about all the variables in your own current situation, as well as consider the long-term advantages and disadvantages of signing a lease. Ask yourself the following questions before you sign a lease:

- Where do you see yourself in a few years?

- Is this an interim setup or something that you perceive as a long-term plan?

- Are you planning on always practicing alone or do you think you might have partners or associates in the future?

Some leases might make it impossible, or at least difficult and costly, to terminate or modify terms before the maturation date. It is not uncommon for some reasonable modification of the lease to be acceptable to the landlord. One such example might be a section in the lease that references the fact that if you leave before the end of the lease term, and you are able to find another health-care provider to take over your lease, you are still responsible for that person. In other words, if you relocate to another country and someone else has taken over your practice and lease, and the person defaults on payment for any reason, or causes damage, then you are still responsible. It would not be unreasonable to add a clause that if you vacate the premises earlier and you are able to find someone who will take over the lease (with the necessary signed documentation) that the new person will be fully responsible for the leased property and related payments, and you will be freed from any further responsibility or cost.

If in doubt, get help with understanding the lease. The safest plan, while it can be quite costly for you, is to get a lawyer to help you with this. In the earlier stages of my career, I thought I was able to handle all these things, but the wiser I became in these domains the more help I sought — particularly with regard to legal advice. Sometimes at the beginning of your career you can feel that you are invincible and can do it all — that is so wrong! Sometimes you need another professional person's help.

Another point is that not all rental situations require a lease, but it's prudent to get something in writing at the outset. The best way for me to illustrate this is to give you an example from my own experience. This came about when I first started practicing as a surgeon and a temporary rental arrangement transpired. While I knew I ultimately wanted my own office, I was not ready for that right after finishing my specialty training.

A more senior medical colleague provided an opportunity for me to set up shop on his premises. This was actually in a building in which the doctors owned their units, so it was not a case where a lease was offered, or needed, by the doctor. All I needed to do was pay a specified amount per month that would cover the working space and some shared services such as the waiting area, photocopier, and printer. This was really appealing and exactly what I needed at that time, with little office outlay expenses, and no long-term obligations.

We were both happy with the arrangement that we had agreed on with our discussions and we were both keen to move forward with me setting up an office. All this planning was done by casual conversation and by means of a "handshake." We didn't have anything in writing — no terms, no minimum stay, and no other points of mutual understanding.

I made sure I at least documented the most pertinent points of the discussions we had during the meetings so misunderstandings would not arise in the future. Everything went really well and I rented from him for three years, all with very little formal contractual documentation. The little we had in writing was enough to ensure we were on the same page, particularly with regard to me giving appropriate notice when vacating the premises so I could leave to set up my own office.

While this scenario went well with no glitches, there can often be animosity, which can result from such a setup in which no formal understanding of the conditions has been appropriately documented. It is for this reason that it is essential that a written formal agreement is in place, just in case things do not go as planned. My situation was rare, and if that situation recurred, I would definitely have done a more structured and formal agreement. It is also a good idea to hire a professional for advice, and with help in executing the agreement.

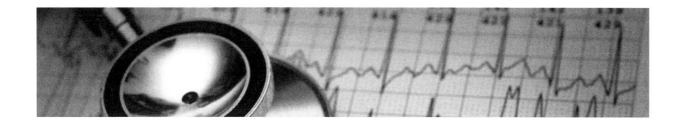

7

THE LEGAL, BUSINESS, AND INSURANCE ASPECTS OF RUNNING A PRACTICE

It is always a good idea to consult with other professionals, such as lawyers and accountants, especially at the beginning of your practice. This chapter will help you make sure you are on the right track with the legal aspects of running your practice right from the start.

1. HIRING A LAWYER AND GETTING LEGAL ADVICE

As has been alluded to, there is always a place for utilizing a lawyer with the initiation and running of a practice. I can provide several examples where I have appreciated the services of a lawyer. First, with the initial lease of a facility, I always think, as mentioned in Chapter 6, that it is prudent to gain some expert help before signing on the dotted line. While many documents are simple, others have all kinds of things embedded in the details that could have

major implications for you. A small financial investment in legal services at the outset can prevent much unpleasantness, and stress, later — which ultimately could be more expensive than if you would have paid a small fee for a legal professional's help in the beginning.

Be sure to do your research in terms of legal fees. The fees can differ immensely from one lawyer to the next, and there might be legitimate reasons for the differences in price, but you should at least be fully informed. With this professional service, it is very important to be open with the lawyer up front and ask how much the maintenance fee will be. It is also better to communicate legal matters in writing, such as over email, rather than verbally as you will always have something to refer back to should there be a query about billing at a later date. I have certainly relied on this type of communication as a back-up on many occasions to clarify a bill that I did not fully understand.

I have utilized the services of a lawyer with regard to the logistics of maintaining a corporation. Different jurisdictions and countries have their own rules in terms of whether a doctor or health professional can incorporate a practice, and what the terms are. This was certainly a situation in which I sought legal counsel, and the associated services, to set up my corporation. (See section **6**. for more information about incorporation.)

Another area in which I have had input from lawyers is with regard to medical litigation coverage and their professional opinions. All doctors and health professionals should have the appropriate protective insurance when practicing medicine. There are sometimes situations that fall outside the boundaries of what you are covered for, without you even being aware of it. The example to follow illustrates this point.

At one point in my career, I was a consultant for an agency that was involved in taking care of musicians while they were on tour in the city I was living at the time. I was fortunate to have met some really big stars in this role. I also got to watch many great shows backstage, which was a real treat. I periodically was called in after hours to take care of the musicians' medical needs, mostly as a result of recent illnesses. I was quite concerned that should anything go wrong, the medical protection insurance that I had at the time was not sufficient to cover me in the case of possible medical litigation. I thus contacted the legal department of the insurance organization responsible for my coverage, and indeed found out that it was necessary for me to purchase additional insurance. The coverage I had did not cover out-of-country patients who did not have an emergency situation. This would mean that if

I continued to be involved in these few medical situations in any given year, I would have to purchase additional litigation insurance if I wished to be appropriately covered for medical services of this nature.

Even though this experience was all very exciting, it was not worth the large extra premium that I was required to pay, for just a few patients per year that fell into this category. Reluctantly, I stopped providing this service because the potential downsides and extra expense far outweighed the fun part of the experience — this was all guided by the legal advice I received.

2. LITIGATION

Doctors and those in related health-care fields can be involved with litigation in so many different ways, other than just being sued! It should be emphasized that health-care professionals should always have the necessary litigation coverage; in fact, it is required in many situations before you are able to work in a health-care setting.

Once again, rather than go through all the logistics, I will provide you with some concrete examples of how this can play out in the real world.

2.1 Consent to release information about a patient in a legal case

For the first example I will tell you about a lawyer's letter I actually received in the mail the day I was writing this portion of the chapter. It was from a law firm in the city where I used to live. A patient had a slip and fall accident a few years ago, and she had legal representation in terms of pursuing the matter further. While I don't know the details of the legal process that was planned, I suspect she was taking action against the facility or organization where the accident occurred, or an insurance company, seeking compensation. I was asked to provide a copy of all the clinical notes present in the file to the legal firm. This letter from the law firm came with the necessary signed consent from the patient that allowed me to forward this information to a third party.

It is worth mentioning at this point that you are not permitted to reveal any patient information to anyone, without prior signed consent from your patient, unless of course it is a police investigation and you are required by law to do so. You are also not allowed to talk to others about a patient, and specifically you are not allowed to reveal any identifying information. This would require patient consent as well if you wanted to mention patient details in any type of conversation other than one with the patient. Being generic in conversation about an occurrence such as the one I have just described is acceptable as long as no identifying information is disclosed.

2.2 Expert consultant for a law firm or insurance company

A second example of an interaction with a lawyer is where a doctor acts as an expert consultant for a law firm or insurance company. Perhaps a patient has a lawyer involved in an appeal case in which compensation was refused from a work-related consequence. The following example explains this in more detail.

Mr. Jake was employed at a construction industry for many years. For the first 10 years he worked with jackhammers, and then as a forklift operator for another 20 years. As a result of the noise exposure over a long period of time he sustained significant hearing loss that requires him to wear hearing aids. In the earlier years of his occupation it was not emphasized that he needed to use adequate ear protection to prevent noise damage.

In addition to the noise that Mr. Jake was exposed to at work, he did some recreational shooting for about five years when he was younger. While completing his Workers' Compensation claim forms, which are quite comprehensive, Mr. Jake is compelled to disclose any other noise exposure in the past, other than work. In fact, there was a specific question about recreational shooting, and if that was ever done. Being an honest man and having oodles of integrity, Mr. Jake did the correct thing and mentioned that he engaged in recreational shooting for five years when he was much younger, but he did wear the necessary ear protection when doing so. His claim was evaluated by the compensation board and was rejected due to the history of recreational shooting; the board considered that much of the damage could have been caused by the shooting. In this situation, Mr. Jake can either accept this fate or he can appeal the situation.

Mr. Jake decides to appeal as both he and his physician feel this decision is wrong, so he hires a lawyer to represent him. The insurance company not only has its regular doctors as consultants but will also have expert physicians, such as a subspecialist (i.e., otologist) who can be brought in for situations like this for additional expert input.

After much stress and expense, Mr. Jake manages to reach a settlement, which in the end covers the legal fees, and leaves a little extra money for him, enough to partially cover the cost of the hearing aids.

2.3 Be aware of the possibility of negligence and malpractice lawsuits

The last type of litigation I wish to cover is something that no physician ever wishes for himself or herself. This is where a patient sues a doctor for negligence, or malpractice. This has become more prevalent worldwide, especially in North America. Sometimes there is a legitimate reason for a patient pursuing litigation against a doctor, but many times there is not. Fortunately, there is a legal system that makes decisions — hopefully having undergone a fair and just process. While there are many stories regarding litigation that I have seen and heard, I would like to tell you about a conversation that will be imprinted in my mind forever.

While I was a medical student, I was on a long-distance flight between North America and Africa. While flying somewhere above the Atlantic Ocean, there was a call on the public announcement system for doctors to identify themselves. I would have thought in a full Boeing 747 there would have been at least one fully qualified doctor on board.

I waited to see if anyone came forward as I was just a medical student. Shortly thereafter they made the same announcement again. I speedily identified myself and told them I was a medical student. They took me to the front of the plane where a middle-aged woman was having heart palpitations. By the time I got there, her heart rate seemed to have slowed down. I did whatever examination I could do under the circumstances and was fortunate that she seemed to settle down; I was not in a position to prescribe medications which the crew actually had available in their emergency kit. I told the airline staff to call me if there were any further concerns, feeling like I had not done much in the situation.

While walking back to my seat a gentleman approached me and asked me about the situation, and whom I was, to which I responded appropriately. It turned out that he was a practicing doctor in the United States and was on his way back to North America. He told me, and I quote, "Young man, if I can give you any advice — don't ever do that again. You will help this patient from the bottom of your heart, and things can go wrong. You can get sued, and while you will probably will not lose the case, you will have to get a lawyer, incur costs, and needless to say endure the stress involved." I was shocked — is this the way some doctors think? I never did take that advice and have always helped people out in emergency medical situations, no matter the venue.

3. HIRING AN ACCOUNTANT

Most people need the services of an expert when it comes to filing tax returns for their practice. I do not recommend taking any shortcuts when it comes to accounting and taxes, particularly if you think that you are going to save money by not using the professional help of an accountant. You will likely save far more money by having your tax returns done by an accountant who knows what he or she is doing, and maximizing on the tax incentives and exemptions that are available to you.

The services that accountants provide are variable, many being involved far beyond the scope of just tax returns. For example, my accountant has provided ongoing advice about all aspects of my practice, including employment and the relevant paperwork, office financial management, and personal investments.

When it comes to setting up and managing your office bookkeeping you can do it yourself, have an employee in your office do the work, or hire an accountant. I have always opted for the accounting firm who does my tax returns to do it all, including the bookkeeping. I provide all the necessary statements, receipts, and other relevant information to the accountant once a year and he takes care of everything — his assistants doing the bookkeeping and himself the more high-level work. This arrangement reassures me to know that this is being taken care of by a person who knows what he is doing! I have also found that my staff concentrate on other aspects of the practice, rather than being swamped with the financial aspects. While this is my preference, it may not be yours. However, it is important to research to see what situation will suit your needs.

4. INVESTMENT ADVISORS

While I do not like to generalize, I can speak for myself and many of the doctors I know — adequate knowledge and experience with investing is not a strength of many physicians. I feel this is something that is far safer left in the hands of people who know what they are doing.

Whether it be an investment specialist with one of the medical associations, an independent investment advisor, an accountant, or even a family member or a friend who is savvy in investment knowledge and strategy, it is way better to get some expert advice than to see your hard-earned money not be wisely, and safely, managed. We all work hard in the health-care professions to earn money, so be careful with how, and with whom, you decide to invest.

Everyone knows too well that the economic climate, and related swings, can affect a person's savings significantly. You have to make tough decisions as to how risky you want your portfolio to be. Personally, I have good and bad stories about investment advisors and the management of my money, but all I can tell you is that it is a matter of personal comfort and trust, and only you will be able to determine who is best to advise you about your finances. Make sure you get expert help and that you feel comfortable with the individual giving it.

5. INSURANCE

There are many different types of insurance you may want, or are required to have, including insurance to cover your office, disability insurance in case you can no longer work, liability and malpractice insurance in case you get sued, and life insurance to help those close to you after you are gone.

5.1 Office insurance

Office insurance is an important consideration that is often overlooked. Do not take for granted that your space and contents within an establishment are covered by the facility insurance — this is often not the case. It is crucial that your office insurance be set up before you take possession of your office space.

Make sure you find and use an insurance company that is familiar with commercial insurance and coverage. Research different insurance agents because insurance premiums can differ from one company to the next. Word-of-mouth is a good method of finding an appropriate insurance broker or firm, so ask your colleagues, or the building management company for some recommendations for insurance agencies or companies.

5.2 Disability and life insurance

Disability and life insurance are essential requirements you need to look into from day one, even if you have a preexisting plan in place. As soon as you start the first day of your career you need to make sure you have adequate coverage should anything untoward happen.

It is better to get disability and life insurance set in stone when you are young and healthy. Once you get older, with possible medical problems, the complexity involved in the application process becomes more of an issue, premiums get higher, and depending on how bad the situation is, coverage may not be possible at all. I personally feel that disability insurance is something that is absolutely needed, and should not be considered as optional. Life insurance is an area where there might be further considerations depending on your own personal situation. Once again this is something that requires expert input from someone who knows what he or she is doing to give you the best possible options.

Just keep in mind that there are personal and work-related disability insurance packages, and you need them both. Personal disability would cover your personal income with a certain amount that you would receive in lieu of a salary or other relevant income. Office insurance would cover your office overhead, which as you can imagine can be exorbitant in some situations. Professional insurance agents in this area will be able to guide you with more information and provide you with suggestions for the best possible coverage for your unique situation.

If you are planning to incorporate your business and you will be receiving dividend income as a shareholder instead of a regular salary, some disability insurance plans will not consider this type of income in their insurable-income calculations. Talk to your disability insurance provider if you are considering incorporating.

For all your insurance needs, make sure you do your homework with regard to your medical-related affiliations. Often there are better rates and plans designed for your needs. These plans are negotiated to be more reasonably priced with a contract in place between the insurance company and the organization, based on bulk sign-ups. Many medical societies and licensing authorities have something like this in place with custom-designed plans specifically geared toward health-care professionals' needs. I certainly get inundated with all kinds of special rates based on memberships with these organizations.

5.3 Liability and malpractice insurance

You need adequate professional liability insurance to protect you and your business in case you get sued. Your medical protective insurance will cover you for potential litigation relating to your professional practice. Often your office insurance will cover if someone, for example, slips and injures himself or herself in your office. You, however, need to make sure you are covered in the event of any type of litigation such as negligence, misrepresentation, violation of good faith, or inaccurate advice.

Speak to experienced people in your field, or get some advice from senior colleagues in a similar practicing field as yourself to ensure your policies are inclusive.

6. INCORPORATING YOUR MEDICAL PRACTICE

Incorporating a medical practice is not always the same as incorporating any other type of business. There are special rules and limitations that apply to medical practices, especially for doctors. Also, the allied health professions have their own regulations about incorporation. Each country, state, and province has different rules about this so it is best that you discuss incorporation with your colleagues and professional advisors such as your accountant and legal professional.

In many states and provinces the following professions may be considered a professional corporation as opposed to a regular business corporation: physicians, surgeons, veterinarians, physiotherapists, psychologists, speech-language pathologists, respiratory therapists, audiologists, podiatrists, chiropractors, dental hygienists, dental surgeons, dental technologists, denturists, dietitians, massage therapists, medical laboratory technologists, medical radiation technologists, nurses, occupational therapists, opticians, and optometrists. Consult with your governing body for the conditions of incorporation specific to your profession and your location.

The following two sections discuss both the American and Canadian incorporation information. The sections are more general in nature because there are so many variations in the different jurisdictions. These sections are meant as an overview. Again, talk to your professional advisors if you are considering incorporation.

6.1 Professional limited liability company (PLLC) in the United States

The professional limited liability company (PLLC) is for businesses that provide professional services (e.g., doctors and chiropractors) that want to incorporate.

Every state has different rules when it comes to forming a PLLC, such as restricting who may be a shareholder or director in the professional corporation. In many cases, company shares must be owned by employees performing the professional services. In some states, only licensed practitioners are allowed to own stocks and serve on the boards of directors; while in other states at least 50 percent of the shareholders and directors must be licensed professionals. In many states, if a shareholder dies, the company may need to disband because of these rules.

There are also strict rules when it comes to naming the corporation. In most areas the name of the corporation has to include the doctor's name and "Professional Corporation." The reason for this is to make sure the name represents what type of corporation it is and the function of the medical practice. As a result

of this, the name of a corporation can be quite lengthy — more than a couple of words!

There are many additional costs to an incorporated business as opposed to a non-incorporated business. For example, start-up costs can be pricey and then the additional work of filing the corporation's tax returns, monthly corporate income tax installments, and the monthly deductions on salaries paid to the employees.

Talk to your governing body or state licensing agency about PLLCs for more information if you are considering incorporating your practice. If you look on the Internet, you will find many links in this regard.

6.2 Incorporation in Canada

It has only been in the last decade or so that legislation has been passed so that doctors can form a corporation in Canada. Most provinces have passed legislation making incorporation an option; however, it is important to check into this in the early stages of your practice setup.

There are also strict rules when it comes to naming the corporation. In most areas the name of the corporation has to include the doctor's name, which means the corporation cannot be a numbered corporation. Also the name may need to include "Professional Corporation" in some jurisdictions. The reason for this is to make sure the name represents what type of corporation it is and the function of the medical practice.

An incorporated medical practice usually obtains a certificate of authorization from the provincial licensing body. This is something to ask about at the time you obtain your provincial licence, or before you set up the office. I found my accountant to be a very valuable source of input when it came to incorporation, and he referred me to a lawyer to get this set up and functioning. (The Resources section on the CD includes some examples.)

There are many additional costs to an incorporated business as opposed to a non-incorporated business. For example, start-up costs and then the additional work of filing the corporation's tax returns, monthly corporate income tax installments, and the monthly deductions on salaries paid to the doctor and employees can be pricey. Here again I suggest getting a second opinion if you find a cost excessive.

There are also costs associated with filing corporation papers that lawyers have no control over. There are, however, significant benefits if you are incorporated, particularly in terms of taxation — this making up for the extra cost incurred with the setting up and running of a corporation.

It cannot be emphasized enough to talk to your accountant, financial advisor, and lawyer about the pros and cons of incorporating your medical practice and to get the specific facts for your area.

For the allied health professions, check with your governing body to see what the rules and regulations are for incorporating your business.

7. ADDITIONAL INFORMATION

Be cognizant of the fact that you may need to get additional registrations set up such as an Employer Identification Number (EIN) in the US, and in Canada, a Business Number (BN). The Resources section on the CD has links to find out more about this.

In North America, each province and state has different requirements for practicing health-care professionals, including for prescribing controlled substances, such as narcotics. Many jurisdictions mandate that these prescriptions have to be written on a special prescription pad, and other checks are carried out during the process, including some onus on the pharmacist. You can imagine that poor prescribing habits, or these prescriptions in the wrong hands, can have a detrimental outcome. We have all heard about situations in which individuals have obtained strong painkillers from more than one source, the result for the patient being tragic. You might also have read or heard about individuals who obtain large quantities of these medications and then sell them on the street or black market.

If your practice is going to be set up to perform laboratory services, you need to consult with the regulatory bodies such as your regional Department of Health and Human Services to ensure you are complying with clinical laboratory guidelines.

Depending on the nature of your practice, a state or provincial tax number will be needed if you are providing taxable services or selling taxable items in your office.

Checklist 3 will help you plan your legal, business, and insurance needs.

LEGAL, BUSINESS, AND INSURANCE ASPECTS OF RUNNING A MEDICAL PRACTICE

1. Do you have an adequate contract relating to the premises? _____

2. Do you have *personal* disability insurance? _____

3. Do you have *practice* disability insurance? _____

4. Do you have life insurance? _____

5. Write down the different places that offer insurance and compare services and costs:

   _____
   _____
   _____
   _____
   _____
   _____
   _____

6. Have you researched potential legal counsel? You may want to write down a list of places you have found and then check the price for the services and compare.

   _____
   _____
   _____
   _____
   _____
   _____
   _____
   _____

7. Do you need to hire an accountant? If so, for what services?

   _____
   _____
   _____
   _____
   _____
   _____
   _____
   _____

8. Do you have an investment advisor? _____

9. What type of practice do you want to have (i.e., corporation or not)? You may want to list the pros and cons of each type of practice to see what situation will suit you.

   _____
   _____
   _____
   _____
   _____
   _____
   _____

10. Do you need to apply for an Employer Identification Number (EIN) or Business Number (BN)?

   _____

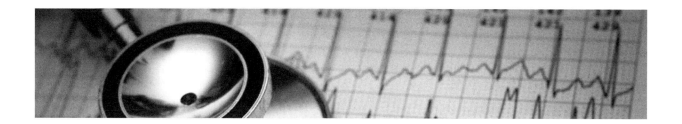

8

EQUIPMENT AND SUPPLIES

Do not rush into buying office equipment, furniture, and supplies. Whether you are setting up an office for the very first time, relocating, or just upgrading a present setup, there is no point spending more money than you need to. Research what's available by asking others where to find the best deals. You can divide your needs into "must have" or "nice to have" lists. This will help you prioritize your long list of needs. One of the things that was really helpful for me was visiting different offices to get an idea of what other offices looked like and how things were set up. As mentioned in the next few paragraphs, I also looked at multiple different sources to see what my best options were.

For the furniture, I found the best prices from a company that specialized in office furniture. There was also a possibility for secondhand furniture at a lesser amount, but the difference in price was negligible and did not make it worth settling for second best.

My medical equipment came from a combination of sources, including medical supply companies, web-based companies, and an office of a colleague who had recently passed away. By being comprehensive and looking at all the different options, I managed to save tens of thousands of dollars on the initial setup.

You can always upgrade later on, but in the beginning it's prudent to be careful with your money and acquire those "must haves" at the best possible price.

I think, first and foremost, for the more expensive items in particular, ask as many people as you can whether they know of a doctor, or similar health-care professional, that is imminently retiring or relocating. Often these professionals are very keen to sell their office equipment and furniture within a short period of time and might be quite flexible with the purchase price.

You should also be researching the Internet for deals. Many people forget to look at the classifieds in medical journals and other medical publications. I always see doctors, and offices, that are advertising office equipment for sale. You may be surprised as to how much you can find on general websites such as eBay.

If you are really lucky, you might even find an office setup that is fully supplied and equipped for you to be able to walk into and take over as a turnkey operation. That was the situation for a newly graduated doctor when I relocated to another part of the country. My colleague took over a fully functional, furnished and equipped office, with a large patient volume already in place. All he had to do from a functional point of view was just walk in and start working!

1. ADHERENCE TO GUIDELINES FOR EQUIPMENT

Whatever you do, do not forget to be familiar with guidelines that might be mandatory for an appropriate office setup. There are certain medical fields, or disciplines, in which you are obliged to comply with regulations with an office setup. One example is a physician who is going to do surgery in his or her office — either as the only location in which he or she performs surgery, or in conjunction with a hospital practice.

If major surgeries will be performed in an office setting, there will usually be accrediting bodies that will impose specific standards of practice on such a setup. The accrediting bodies stipulate minimum requirements be present to run a safe practice, and they will even make visits to your premises to make sure everything has been done to comply with acceptable guidelines. The guidelines are for the benefit and safety of your patients, albeit they can be a significant inconvenience and stress factor for you, your staff, and the organization in general.

2. TECHNOLOGY

Acquiring up-to-date computers and compatible printers is important in order to run the necessary medical programs. Also, investing in programs such as MS Excel or some accounting program will help if an administrator decides to do the bookkeeping for the office.

There are software programs that specialize in calendars and booking abilities; these programs are specifically geared toward a medical-type practice. Some of the best places to find out about medical-related computer programs are in the classifieds in publications from medical associations or societies. The companies and programs in the classifieds are geared more toward a local environment. By doing web-based research you will find many references for such companies by entering relevant key words.

While antivirus software and firewall protection for your computer(s) might be a given, do make sure you have the appropriate security for your computer system. If you are using wireless connections, have the relevant barriers to secure your network. This is the time that if you, or someone else around you, does not have good computer skills and troubleshooting ability, to get a professional to organize your computer files and system. I have certainly made use of computer experts with my more complex computer setups and problem solving.

When it comes to the rest of your technology needs, you have to decide on the basics needed to function in your office, while keeping long-term goals in mind, as well as how much extra cost you are willing to absorb. Facsimile machines, photocopiers, label printers, automated prescription printers, and more are all options that you need to look at, both from a short- and long-term point of view. You can spend hundreds or thousands of dollars, depending on your needs and preferences. My advice is to spend a little more at the outset, rather than having to upgrade after a year or two, which would turn out to be more costly in the end. I also encourage you, on the more expensive purchases, to ensure that you have extended warranties, as repairs on these items can be quite costly.

Depending on the nature of the office and whether you accept cash, debit card, or credit card transactions for services provided, you will have to acquire further software and machines for processing theses charges.

3. PHONE SYSTEM

Obtaining a phone system for your office is one situation in which you will become wiser through experience, but some basic information at the outset does not hurt. One thing I learned for the phone system in my clinical office was not to cut corners and save money for the sake of a cheaper but inferior setup. Spending that little extra cost up front can make life so much easier for you and your staff in the long run. I almost opted for the less-expensive version, but I am so happy that I paid the extra amount for the convenience of the superior setup.

The possibilities are immense in terms of options for your phone system. Music and customized messages while on hold, rollover provisions, automated operators, intercom systems, paging systems, and voice-mail preferences are just a few of the things that you have to consider with your phone package. These always come with a price, but more often the extra cost for some of these features are worth every extra cent invested. The options for features that you can include for a telephone package are immense. Be sure to research all your options, ask lots of questions, and utilize the experts at the different companies you contact.

There are also possibilities for purchasing versus leasing a system, and each has their own benefits and drawbacks. I opted for the purchasing option after much consultation and thought. It seemed that a five-year lease term cost almost as much as the initial outlay if I was going to buy it outright. I decided to purchase the system because then it was fully paid for, and it belonged to me. The only downside seemed to be that upgrading to a new system would have been expensive. With the lease option, I would have had the ability to switch to newer technology once the lease had expired.

Very recently I was involved in a relocation of an administrative office. The move required a whole new phone system. While I, and my staff, had a reasonably good idea of what we wanted, when we received the assessment and opinion by the expert, things changed a lot with the new setup based on the recommendations.

This type of technology is forever changing and the experts are up-to-date with the most advanced systems available. I highly recommend you speak to an expert before choosing a system for your office.

4. FURNITURE

Most medical and allied health offices will need chairs, desks, cupboards, filing cabinets, bookcases, examining tables, or in the case of massage therapists and chiropractors, special apparatus to lie down on. These need to be custom designed to whatever practice is being set up — the needs differ immensely from one health-care profession to the next.

Also, with chairs, most places are switching to easy-to-wash chairs that don't have cloth material. Instead it is vinyl or some similar plastic material. There are hospitals that are also modifying their furniture because of the expense of keeping cloth material clean and unstained.

Infectious diseases are becoming a challenge in public places and particularly health-care settings. A good example of this is the recent H1N1 influenza outbreak and the modifications that have resulted from this. Hand-washing and hand sanitizers are being used more than ever. Some offices no longer allow magazines in the waiting rooms due to the H1N1 outbreak. As a result offices have resorted to alternative means of keeping people busy while they are waiting, including TVs with health-related trivia information going across the screen, or having a news channel such as CNN on with no sound and closed-captioning. Also, many dentists now have TVs mounted in the ceiling or above the patient's chair with a remote control wrapped in easy-to-clean plastic, so patients can watch TV while getting their teeth cleaned.

Some offices also choose to have health-brochure stands for holding many different types of brochures related to common illnesses or injuries.

5. DESTROYING CONFIDENTIAL FILES

There are different options for shredding confidential documentation. If you have an electronic office, disposing of confidential information is less of a problem — yet another reason to consider a paper-free office. For lesser amounts of paper, you can purchase a relatively inexpensive paper shredder and do it yourself. I have done this before, but I have found these machines quite temperamental, especially the inexpensive ones.

What I have utilized more of are companies that specialize in shredding. There are those that bring a shredding van or equipment to your office, or take it to another location for shredding. I have utilized both of these services, although I find the onsite shredding more convenient.

6. STATIONERY

You have several options for stationery in the office. Depending on the system in your office, this might be less of an issue at the time of setup. Even if you have an electronic office you will still need prescription pads, letterheads, etc. For those who wish to have this all automated through your computer system, you will just need the basic paper supplies. For those health-care providers who prefer customized letter heads and prescription pads, you will have to arrange this through a printing company. This is another one of those things that you will have to arrange ahead of time.

Another handy tool that I only discovered after I started a practice, are customized stamps. One of them I used in the office for prescriptions, with the signature and required registration number on the stamp. I stamped the prescription pads ahead of time, thus saving that extra time when completing prescriptions. Be sure you keep these in a safe place, and not in easy vision of patients. You will be surprised what patients can remove from your office when you leave for a few moments. Signed prescription pads are very valuable in the wrong hands, and fraud is not unknown when it comes to fake prescriptions for medications such as narcotics. Some jurisdictions will have extra screening mechanisms and rigor in place when you prescribe narcotics, but some will not — so be familiar with this concept, if that is part of your clinical practice.

The other stamps I have used frequently were in the hospital, at times where forms or prescriptions needed to be completed. The stamps had relevant information including my name, credentials, and contact details. I also had a stamp that was designed specifically for completing a prescription. It had all the frequent medications that I prescribed after surgery. All I had to do was fill in the dose, and cross out the ones that did not apply. The pharmacists certainly appreciated it, as doctors' handwriting is not always the best!

There are lots of choices when it comes to ordering office supplies such as pens, paper, etc. From my experience in many different settings, I have tried to simplify it as much as possible. I have also given the responsibility of obtaining office supplies to an office administrator, except for the bigger and more expensive purchases. For these more significant and costly items, I have found that making a trip to one or more stores gives me a better idea of possibilities before committing.

For the smaller purchases, ordering from a catalog every month, or biweekly, and having it delivered to the office has made the most sense to me and my staff. While there are office supply retailers who specialize in this type of thing, make sure to find out if you are eligible for a corporate or group discount with suppliers.

7. OFFICE CLEANING SUPPLIES

A medical supply company from which you receive your regular medical supplies, instruments, and equipment, usually has a selection of cleaning supplies for all your office needs.

Most importantly, you need to make sure the cleaning supplies that are used are safe for patients, staff, and yourself. There are solutions that you can obtain for your instrumentation that can be quite toxic if not used as suggested.

Some solutions require a ventilation system for use, to avoid harmful fumes being circulated. These supply companies usually have a sales representative, or customer service person, who can help you with this type of advice. Consulting with facilities where this is used on a frequent basis, such as a hospital outpatient setting with similar cleaning procedures, will be a good resource for your questions.

8. NOTICES AND SIGNS FOR PATIENTS TO READ WHILE WAITING

Signage for the exterior of the office is covered in Chapter 6. For signs that will be inside your practice, you can choose to use the same kind of specialized signage business, or you can make signs through a printing company with something less expensive, but not as durable.

Computers usually have programs that allow you to design and print reasonable looking signs, that will suffice if this is a temporary notice, or something that needs to be replaced periodically.

Your signs may be there to help remind patients about noise, cell phone use, and consuming refreshments in your office — it is not a given that patients will consider these factors if they are important to you. Make some simple and friendly notices to put up in visible places in the office so patients know the "office rules."

9. GENERAL MEDICAL SUPPLIES

Many basic office supplies are common to all health-care professionals, examples being antibacterial soaps, liquid sanitizers, paper towels, and facial tissue. Some professionals require items such as throat swabs, gloves, masks, paper for exam tables, syringes, and needles. Other offices will need more specific supplies such as specimen bottles, suction equipment, and examination lamps to name a few. The lists are lengthy and vary significantly from one health-care profession to the next. Make sure you visit another office, where a similar practice is on the go already, and make detailed notes as to all you need to get for your office.

Your professional association will usually provide you with some information for your office needs. Do not forget to contact the sales representatives with medical supply companies; these agents usually have a wealth of knowledge in this domain, particularly if they have been around in the business for a while.

One thing that I was not fully prepared for was to have a supply of the basic medications that are needed when assessing patients in my field in the office setting. Ointments, eye drops, ear drops, and similar items that can be readily applied in the office should always be on hand.

Checklist 4 gives you an example of what you may need to acquire for your office setup. You may find yourself adding more items as you get closer to the start date. This is totally normal as you simply cannot remember everything, or predict additional items, until you actually start with the whole process. Not being diligent, structured, and comprehensive with this step will result in you forgetting things, duplication, inefficiency, and ultimately wasting your time and money. The CD also includes a copy of this checklist.

CHECKLIST 4
OFFICE EQUIPMENT AND SUPPLIES

Technology

Do you need the following? (You may also want to list which warranties have extended coverage included, or options for increasing the coverage.)

☐ Computers (How many will you need for your office? Optimal hardware, software, networking, ability for facsimile, etc.)

_____

_____

☐ Facsimile machine
☐ Photocopier
☐ Label printer
☐ Automated prescription printers
☐ Debit card and credit card machine
☐ Cash register

(Please note, for most of the above-listed items, they can be purchased stand-alone or in combination — it depends on how your office is going to function.)

What type of computer software programs do you need?

☐ Medical records and patient information program (You may want to list some of the programs you have come across to help you with your search for the right program for your office.)

_____

_____

_____

_____

_____

_____

☐ Patient-booking software
☐ Antivirus software
☐ Accounting programs
☐ Billing software
☐ Other: _____
☐ Other: _____

What have you come across in your research for a telephone system?

_____

_____

_____

_____

Furniture

Depending on your type of practice, you may need all or some of the following:

☐ Number of chairs you will need for the —
   ☐ waiting room
   ☐ examination rooms
   ☐ staff area
   ☐ your office
☐ Other area: _____

☐ Number of desks you will need for the —
   ☐ waiting room
   ☐ examination rooms
   ☐ staff area
   ☐ your office
   ☐ Other area: _____
☐ Cabinets for exam rooms (or other areas in the office)
☐ Filing cabinets (How many?): _____
☐ Bookcases (How many?): _____
☐ Side tables
☐ Beds or examination tables (How many?): _____
☐ Footstools for children and elderly (to get on examination bed)
☐ Container for umbrellas in the waiting room
☐ Hanging space or jacket rack
☐ Mat for boots or shoes for winter and rainy seasons
☐ Magazine rack
☐ Brochure rack
☐ Rack or table for children's items
☐ Other: _____
☐ Other: _____

General Office Supplies

☐ Paper shredder or hire a specialized paper shredding company
☐ Bins for confidential shredding
☐ Stationery (pens, paper, etc.)
☐ Customized stamps
☐ Prescription pads
☐ Cleaning supplies
☐ Garbage bins
☐ Bins for recyclables
☐ Bins for confidential shredding
☐ Kitchen supplies if applicable
☐ Other: _____
☐ Other: _____

Medical Supplies

☐   Specimen bottles
☐   Suction equipment
☐   Examination lamp
☐   Wall-mounted equipment
☐   Diagnostic equipment
☐   Stethoscope
☐   Blood pressure cuff
☐   Supplies and equipment for a medical emergency
☐   Syringes and sharps
☐   Sharps container
☐   Sterilization solutions
☐   Sterilization unit
☐   Appropriate covers for bed (paper rolls)
☐   Covers for patients who need to be unclothed for exams
☐   Swabs, sponges, and alcohol wipes
☐   Laboratory investigation supplies
☐   Cleaning supplies
☐   Any medications relevant to your clinical field that are needed in the office setting
☐   Other: _____
☐   Other: _____

Other Miscellaneous Supplies

☐   Antibacterial soaps
☐   Liquid sanitizers
☐   Paper towels
☐   Facial tissue
☐   Children's books and toys
☐   Pictures for the walls
☐   Office rules signs
☐   Window coverings if applicable
☐   Washroom supplies if applicable
☐   Other: _____
☐   Other: _____

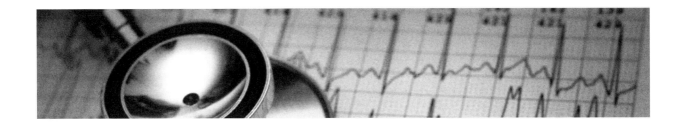

9

HIRING EMPLOYEES

This chapter will help you get started with your hiring process. It will cover the basics of finding and interviewing employees, checking references, salary and benefits, and staff contracts.

1. HIRING OPTIONS

When it comes to hiring staff, the first decision you will need to make is how many people you will need to hire. What might be ideal for your set-up could turn out to be very costly for you. Therefore, you have to carefully consider what you can afford, and what you can't do without, when it comes to your staffing needs in the beginning. The following sections discuss the different types of hiring options you may have when you are first starting out.

1.1 Contract services

There are so many services available where you can contract out services, thereby reducing the number of staff that you actually need to employ. This option, if done wisely, can reduce the expenses significantly.

For example, depending on the type of practice you have and what your transcription preferences and needs are, you have different options. Many health-care providers are very much in the routine of dictating consultation letters or other clinic notes for every patient visit. Having an extra staff member whose primary responsibility is typing clinical notes might be an unnecessary expense. There are transcription services readily available where you can contract your typing for a significantly lower expense than it would cost you for another full-time, or even part-time, employee.

In addition, there are voice-recognition software programs that require less staff than would be otherwise needed with the conventional typing route. These systems are based on voice recognition, automatically typing the note while you are talking on the phone or into some other Dictaphone device. Just be aware that these systems still need some "human input" as they have to be reviewed and edited by someone. Errors are not uncommon with this mode of dictation, and you do not want reports going out that are inaccurate, misleading, or just plain sloppy.

1.2 Whether or Not to Hire Staff with Experience

Another consideration is whether to hire staff with experience in the area of your office practice, or perhaps someone you prefer more who has no experience in a similar professional setting. This is not an easy decision to make, but there are benefits and downsides to both options. Having experienced staff when you are just starting out has the benefit of you worrying less about training and not spending the associated time with training. There is also the likelihood of a higher pay scale with someone experienced, as opposed to a less experienced person. There is also the flip side whereby more experienced staff will be set in their ways and less willing to learn new routines, whereas someone new and just out of school will be easier to train to your way of doing things in your office. However, be aware that a new graduate with little experience in the real world will likely not know what to do in unfamiliar, high-stress situations, whether it be patient related, or regarding the volume of work involved.

There are colleges that offer diploma or similar programs for individuals interested in becoming a medical office assistant (MOA). What the person learns at school might not be what actually goes on in your type of medical office. Certainly many people do come into a medical office assistant position without having formal training in this area. Obviously the best option for your first choice of employee is experience and compatibility, which aren't always easy to find.

1.3 Hiring family or friends

Having family or friends work in your office has is benefits and setbacks. First, if you have a smaller office with only one or two employees, unexpected sick time or other leaves of absence can have a big impact on the functioning of the office. Getting a temporary employee at the last minute who is unfamiliar with your office could be just as challenging. So having a family member or friend familiar with your office help out at the last minute can save the day. Having close family on the payroll can also have financial benefits, keeping the money "in the same pot" so to speak.

The downside of having family or friends in the office is the impact it can have on the other employees. I certainly have seen some animosity when a spouse of a physician has been actively involved in the office, particularly when the spouse is in an office manager role. Many health-care professionals choose not to have that close personal and work interaction, for the fear that it might impact on their marriage, or whatever personal relationship. I have also seen a situation in which a family member has been employed in an office and expected to be paid more than the going rate, leading to a feeling of resentment.

2. WHERE TO FIND EMPLOYEES

There are multiple sources you can tap into in order to find new staff for your office. Personally, I have found word-of-mouth, and referrals, the best options for finding employees. I have asked colleagues, hospital employees, friends, and family if they know of someone who is seeking a position who would make a good fit for the office. There are no doubt procedures you have to go through for employing someone new, especially if you are working in an environment in which unions are in place.

Other sources for finding employees include hospital bulletin boards, professional magazines and journals, newspapers, and the Internet.

3. INTERVIEWING POTENTIAL EMPLOYEES

The interview process can be as simple or complex as you wish it to be. In certain environments it will have to be structured with the same questions being asked to all candidates. If you do not follow the required hiring guidelines, you could be challenged by an individual who does not get the job. In certain situations, such as a university or hospital environment, you might have to hire an employee based on seniority, or other similar factors. Make sure you research these points before you commence the search and interviews.

You might choose to do the interview one-on-one with the interviewee or you may want to have you and another staff member interview the person. You could also do a panel interview in which a few staff members are present during the interview. Having a series of short interviews, just like speed dating, or multiple mini-interviews as known in the MD application world, is also not uncommonly used these days.

You can format it as an informal discussion, a semi-structured interview, or completely structured without veering off the scripted questions. Some employers might ask for a five-minute presentation by the candidate outlining his or her reasoning for applying for the position, or what the person's vision for the role is. You can request this beforehand, or ask the candidate to do this on the day of the interview. I know of employers who actually give the interviewee an administrative or clerical task to perform at the time of the interview and see how the person fares in the situation. An example could be providing a file with some different documents, and asking how he or she would deal with each scenario. Whatever format you choose to conduct, make sure it is a friendly environment, and not a situation in which you are out to get the interviewee!

In terms of qualities you are looking for, you should decide in your mind, on paper, or on a computer, your priorities. Some of these characteristics can include interpersonal skills, communication abilities, professionalism, judgment, problem-solving skills, knowledge of the field, ability to think on the spot, self-confidence, and willingness to learn.

Never forget the basics, particularly relating to human rights. You cannot ask questions, amongst others, relating to age, gender, ethnicity, marital status, sexual orientation, or disabilities.

Sample 1 includes the types of questions that can be asked during a job interview. The CD also includes a list of these questions.

INTERVIEW QUESTIONS

1. Tell us something about yourself.

2. Why are you interested in this position?

3. What do you know about the job?

4. What makes you think you are the ideal candidate?

5. Can you give us an example of a challenging work situation you have encountered and how you dealt with it?

6. Can you give us an example of a conflict situation you have experienced, and how you dealt with it?

7. How would you summarize your strengths and weaknesses?

8. Tell us about your strengths and weaknesses in your present or past position.

9. *Mention some real situations that have occurred in your office environment, or could occur, and see how the candidate would deal with the challenge.*

10. What do you think your best friend would say about you?

11. What do you think a fellow employee would say about you?

12. What do you think your references will say about you?

13. Why should you get this position and not the other candidates?

14. If you do get this position, when are you able to start?

15. Are there any planned vacations, or other prolonged absences, planned in the near future?

16. Is there anything you would like to add?

17. Do you have any questions?

18. Do you have any final comments?

4. CHECKING REFERENCES

References are an important aspect of any employee search and hiring process, unless the person is well known within the environment where he or she is seeking a new position. It is not uncommon for someone internal within the facility to apply for an alternate position in the same setting, particularly if this involves a more senior role. References can be obtained at any time during the process, but from my experience, most situations involve references being asked for around the time of the interview, or after a successful interview is completed and final decisions are being made.

Three references are the most common amount that are requested, although I have seen as few as two, to as many as four. I have also seen requests for references from a variety of sources such as from a previous employer, a coworker, and a friend. It all depends on the circumstances around the position and the preferences of the search team or employer.

The method of reference letters also varies quite a lot. Some employers prefer to provide a standard template for completion, while others will allow some latitude for a personalized reference letter. Some others, and I have seen this quite often, prefer a telephone conversation with the reference versus a document. The advantage of this is that sometimes more candor will be expressed on the phone versus in writing. The disadvantage of such method of review is that you have nothing formal to show others, or for future reference, other than some notes you have made. Sometimes you will find people unwilling to put something in writing if that is what is required, or unwilling to say it out loud if they are requested to provide a reference by phone. You will have to decide how to handle these situations, particularly if you are very interested in a candidate.

Whatever method you utilize for reference checks, there should be consistency, fairness, and rigor. In some situations, a decision can be challenged, and you may need to show that due diligence was undertaken.

5. SALARY

Staff salary is tricky when you set up your practice. While everyone wants to pay their employees good salaries, it might not be practical or feasible for you to do so in the beginning stages of your practice.

You should ask around in your area, particularly from your colleagues who have similar practices, as to the going rate for staff. There are also many pay scales you can find on the Internet by simply typing in key words that match your type of employee and practice. Certainly for public establishments, there is much transparency as to what staff are paid in a region or institution. Do some web browsing and you will be surprised at the amount of information available. It is also not a bad idea to ask the candidate, especially one that you are close to hiring, as to what the expectation is for a salary, or at least a range.

My first medical office assistant (MOA) was a perfect fit for the position. I chose her after the selection process. While I knew this was the right person to hire, I was also aware that, at the outset, I could not pay a large salary. First, I had to keep finances down, and second, I wanted to leave lots of room for raising the salary in the future, keeping in mind that this was hopefully a long-term employee situation.

After some discussion and negotiation, she understood about having a lower salary initially with the understanding that once I got busy, things would change incrementally.

Things did change through the years so I gradually increased her salary, and after close to ten years in this practice, her income almost doubled.

Paying your staff adequately is the key to keeping your employees long term. More important than money is how you treat them. It goes without saying that if you are not respectful of your employees, or do not have a supportive environment, no money will retain your staff. They need to be made to feel comfortable and happy working in the office.

6. BENEFITS

Keeping staff that functions really well in your practice is crucial. Providing benefits as part of the package is one of those areas in which your staff will appreciate the position that much more. I believe it is worth every cent you spend in offering perks like benefits to keep your valued staff from leaving.

The most common benefits that are included in an employment situation are dental and medical insurance. Disability and life insurance are less commonly offered or provided by employers, but certainly something that can be included in the big picture.

Another example of where you can provide extra effort to make your staff feel appreciated is to cover expenses such as a cell phone. In my practice, I often called my assistant on her cell phone involving work-related matters. Thus, I personally felt that covering her mobile phone expenses was an added benefit, or bonus, for her.

Another point, which I believe is very worthwhile when you have a long-time assistant you obviously trust, is allowing him or her some latitude when purchasing office supplies. I provided my assistant with a supplemental credit card for office purposes. That way she could get needed items at her convenience, and

without the need to use her own money and later deal with the hassle of reimbursement. These small things will definitely make your staff feel valued and trusted, things that should never be underestimated.

Some last things, which should not be overlooked, are bonuses and acknowledgment of special occasions. I always provided a generous salary bonus for the holidays, as well as offered a gift of some sort for birthdays. These gestures make the difference between someone who "likes" the job, to someone who "loves" the job!

7. STAFF CONTRACTS

Staff contracts can be a very inconsistent area when it comes to medical offices. On the one end of the spectrum you can have a formal contract that both parties have to sign, while on the other end you can have a gentlemen's (informal) agreement with work commencing, and proceeding, without any formal paperwork or conditions.

When I employed staff, my contractual arrangements were somewhere in between these two extremes. I had a letter drafted, with the help of my accountant (this could be drawn up with help from a lawyer too), which outlined the terms of employment. This way the employee and I both had something to refer back to, should either of us have any questions along the way. There were no problems that necessitated us having to refer to these forms, but at least we both had the paperwork as a backup.

8. EMPLOYMENT RULES AND REGULATIONS

Whatever method of paperwork you decide to go with, you need to be cognizant of what employment rules and regulations are in place, particularly relating to your geographic jurisdiction. It is not an optimal situation when, down the road, you decide to make some changes related to employment, only to find out the implications, or consequences. You could have been aware of these in the beginning. It is better to find out the employment rules and regulations before you make an employment obligation, rather than after the fact.

Be aware that a verbal offer of employment is generally as good as a written contract; many people think that the written contract is all that counts.

One example of a good time to be aware of the rules might be when you are considering relocating your practice, or terminating your staff. Depending on where you are, and how long your employees have worked for you, whether you like it or not, you will be responsible for a payout. This is often related to the number of years that the employee has been working with you. There may also be unions that represent employees, which are organizations set up for the best interests of your employees.

9. TRAINING THE STAFF

The spectrum of experience and background of your new staff is going to be very varied. Also, your expectations of the person you so carefully hired might be very different from what you actually get. If you are lucky, you might have staff in your practice that are totally familiar with the type of practice you are about to embark on. More than likely, you will have someone that is not completely familiar with the appropriate knowledge of how things are run.

When I started my solo practice, my primary medical office assistant had the necessary background and general training to be well equipped for the job, but had no experience in the specifics of my medical specialty. I made sure she spent some time in another like-minded office to observe, and learn, as much as she could about the logistics of administrating such an office. Having your staff member spend a couple weeks in someone else's office to gain skills relevant to your specialty, at your expense, is a good investment. This plan certainly helped my situation when I opened my first office and my primary office assistant was not experienced in the running of such a specialty office. The tips she learned from the day-to-day goings on of the office of a senior colleague were well worth the time, effort, and expense involved with arranging this. If something like this is unavailable to you, you are going to have to spend more time working together to get things running smoothly, especially before you open the doors for business. You might also have to rely on further training courses for your staff at the outset.

Professional development is very important, both for the good of your practice and for the benefit of the employees. Courses that are valuable for your office staff could involve topics such as advanced computer skills, dealing with difficult patients, conflict resolution, billing practices, and accounting skills. This is well-spent money and the benefits are enormous for all involved, particularly when you are trying to set up a successful practice.

Checklist 5 will help you keep organized when you are in the process of hiring employees. The checklist is also included on the CD.

HIRING EMPLOYEES

Staff Hiring

☐ How many employees do I need: _____

☐ Are there other options for contracting out services: _____

☐ Are there dictation software programs that would work for my practice: _____

☐ I have decided to hire an experienced individual(s)

☐ I have decided to hire someone/people new to this type of work

Salary

☐ Is it possible to leave room for raising salary from the initial amount: _____

☐ Is the salary competitive for this type of job: _____

☐ Has the salary been discussed adequately with the potential employee?

Benefits

☐ Can I afford to offer the following benefits?

    ☐ Medical and Dental

    ☐ Disability and life insurance

☐ Can I offer other types of benefits?

    ☐ Cell phone

    ☐ Signing privileges or supplemental credit cards

    ☐ Other: _____

Staff Contracts

☐ Should I offer staff contracts?

☐ Will I need to hire an accountant or lawyer for the staff contracts?

☐ Am I up-to-date on employee rights and unions?

☐ Have I formalized the offer and terms of employment adequately with the potential employee(s)?

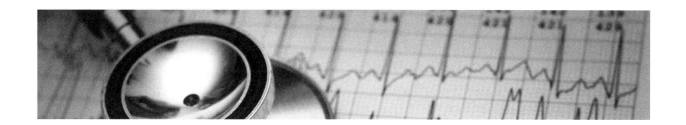

10

HOW TO GET YOUR FIRST PATIENTS

Getting your patients set up and all ready to go from day one of your new office is no easy task and something that can be overlooked very easily. While you are actively getting the logistics figured out for the setup of your new office, start thinking about how you are going to book in patients so there is actually work at hand once you open the doors for the first time.

1. ADVANCE PREPARATION

Before you can even book patients in, you need to get the word out that you are soon hanging out your shingle and will be open for business. Depending on the location and the demand for services in the area, this task might be complex or cumbersome, or not a big deal especially if demand far outweighs supply.

There are so many different ways to let people know how you are commencing a new practice, or modifying an existing practice. Let me give you some context for this from my own experience setting up a solo practice for the very first time. The following sections discuss some of the things I did to facilitate the booking of patients for my new practice. Chapter 11 will give you some additional ideas for promoting your business.

1.1 Word of mouth

I spoke to as many people as I could to help spread the word that I was opening up a new office soon. I carried business cards at all times, so that I could readily provide people with contact information, of course at appropriate venues and circumstances.

As a specialist who had a referral-only practice, I had as many hallway conversations as I could with primary care physicians, introducing myself, and letting them know what medical services I could offer for their patients. At educational rounds, I also interacted with staff and colleagues in a similar fashion.

As a primary-care health professional, the opportunities are somewhat more diverse as to how you can spread the word. Family, friends, colleagues, and others can help with information dissemination.

1.2 Personal visits

I stopped by as many offices I could, targeting practices that would likely refer patients to me. In addition to the doctors, who I tried hard to meet personally, I also spoke to the support staff at the doctors' offices, as they are closely involved with the referral process too.

A personal visit to other offices is something that cannot be underestimated. I left relevant information such as business cards and brochures at each location. (See Chapter 11 for more information about advertising through brochures and business cards.) While this is of most importance for a referral-type practice, meeting local doctors and office staff can be just as beneficial for primary care physicians who do not rely on referring doctors for their practice. Many patients ask doctors, particularly specialists and their office staff, if they are aware of any new primary care physicians who are accepting new patients.

This means of networking is not only important within one health-care profession, but inter-professionally too. As a chiropractor, you might want to say hi to local medical doctors, massage therapists, and others, indicating that you are there to assist with their patients if the need arises.

A new optometrist might make a visit to the local ophthalmologist, informing him or her about the new practice and that an association would be welcome (i.e., cross-referrals between the two fields).

The midwife can make a visit to obstetricians, and family doctors interested in obstetrics, and let them know if they need any help that he or she is around, and discuss referral options.

These are just a few examples, and this type of collegiality exists across all health-care fields.

Some professionals will not pursue such interaction due to competition for services, but I have always believed in the team approach, and you will have to decide what is best for your situation. If you encounter situations in which competition, insecurity, and jealousy are rampant — don't let these attitudes set you back. However, you might have to analyze the situation more carefully and see where your energy is best spent. This is where asking advice from senior colleagues you can trust will aid you immensely. It is always unfortunate when you have to work in an environment that is not too friendly, but this is reality in any line of work — competition and jealousy will always be prevalent in any group of individuals. Keep your head up and just proceed with the task at hand, and do not get caught up in any negative energy around you.

1.3 Notice boards

With my experience, I did some asking around as to possibilities of putting up an announcement on a notice board. It so happened there was an opportunity to do this in the doctor's lounge at the hospital. I certainly made use of this venue for getting the word out, as I knew many doctors frequented the doctor's lounge to pick up their mail and mingle with colleagues.

If you decide to use notice boards to announce your practice, make sure you include all the relevant information and contact details. Details to make sure you include are your area of expertise, services offered, date your practice is opening, office hours, address, phone number, fax number, and possibly email address (or website). You may also want to attach some business cards, or tear-offs, to the notice.

1.4 Mass mailings

Some organizations will allow you to access their mail server, or listings, to send out an announcement to a specific group of caregivers. Others will actually do it for you if you provide the pertinent information to them, which they in turn will forward to the relevant people. It could be a hospital, society, or an association that you belong to that might offer such a service.

One thing to be cognizant of is that it is going to the correct group of people. Most organizations have provisions, or systems in place, for limiting the mailings to a certain group for people based on factors such as area of clinical domain and geography. Make use of these opportunities whenever possible, and go looking for them as they will not look for you!

1.5 Presentation at relevant venues

Depending on your area of expertise, or interest, there might be opportunities to do a presentation at an appropriate event or function. This way you can educate your fellow physicians or health-care providers, while letting them know you have arrived in town and are willing to take part in the care of their patients.

If you are a primary care physician, it is conceivable that there are community or public settings in which you can enlighten people on something related to the medical field. This way you are doing something helpful, yet at the same time you are able to let people know that you are accepting patients in your new practice. These types of events are often well received, sometimes attracting large crowds.

One thing you always have to keep in mind is there are often strict rules and regulations relating to self-promotion and advertising. Make sure you check with your licensing body, or other similar organization, to make sure you are permitted to proceed with such initiatives, and to check what the boundaries are. Getting into trouble with the medical authorities early on in your career, or any time for that matter, is not wise.

1.6 Being available

One of the most appreciated qualities needed of a new physician, or other health-care professional, is being readily available, and willing to help patients, colleagues, and other allied health professionals in any way possible. Developing unnecessary barriers, or indifference at the outset could prove very costly for you in terms of professional ties within the community you are just starting out in. A not-so-charming reputation could also spread amongst the patient population and prospective patients will be reluctant to come and see you!

2. DON'T RUSH PATIENT VISITS

Every discipline, and scope of medical practice, requires different appointment times for consultations and follow-up visits. New patient visits require more time than follow-up visits, unless a procedure or investigation is done at the same time as the follow-up visit, or if the follow-up visit is very complex and requires more than the usual time allocation. In addition, everyone has his or her own style and speed as to how much time is needed with each patient.

The worst thing you can do is rush a visit, particularly in the beginning of your career or in a new practice. Besides doing a potential injustice to the patient, it will not help your reputation which is crucial when you are starting your practice.

Personally, one of the things that I have learned with time is that rushing through a clinic does not help anyone. It can make the patient feel less important at the time of the short visit, stress out your office staff unnecessarily, and put you in a bad mood for having to move so rapidly through things. I think this is a big factor when it comes to job satisfaction — spending adequate time with your patients and not being perpetually rushed is really important.

Having said that, there will be unforeseen situations in which you get really backed up. Patients will have no alternative but to wait longer than usual in the waiting room before seeing you. It should be mentioned at this point that it is better to spend a little longer with a problem situation, than to hasten someone out before an adequate resolution is met. This fine balance of more time spent with one patient, yet delaying the rest of your patients, will be more familiar to you with time, and you will be able to devise your own style of dealing with these types of situations.

3. DAILY SCHEDULE

Scheduling differs immensely from one type of health-care provider to the next. In fact, the daily schedule in two practitioners' offices that deal with exactly the same type of problems can look very different.

I have modified my own schedule through the years, now almost seeing half the number of patients per day than I processed during the earlier stages of my career. Sample 2 is an example of what a daily schedule might look like for a doctor. Note that different professions may have different time frames for dealing with patients; for example, a massage therapist may schedule a patient every hour and have ten minutes between each appointment to clean up the room and prepare for the next patient. Naturally, in the beginning you are going to have more new patient visits than follow-ups so make sure to schedule appropriately.

4. DEALING WITH PATIENTS THAT MISS APPOINTMENTS

Patients not showing up for appointments are a challenging situation for clinics. These account for gaps in your schedule, other patients potentially not having had an opportunity to see you due to a long waiting list, and lost income (depending on your funding plan).

Medical offices deal with this in so many different ways, depending on multiple factors. Options include billing a patient for not showing up, overbooking a clinic to compensate for no-shows, or doing nothing about it. I actually welcome the odd break when a patient does not show for an appointment, allowing me to catch up on things during that free time.

If a patient doesn't show for an hour-long appointment, which does occur in some areas of clinical medicine, this could have a major impact on the day. Also, if there are several no-shows, however short the appointments, this once again could affect the practice flow immensely. This is why many health professionals' offices bill patients if they don't show up for appointments, or if they cancel at the last minute. Many offices provide some information up front as to how long before the appointment a person can cancel without penalty. If you are going to charge for no-shows, it is absolutely necessary to alert patients beforehand and educate them about any penalty.

The strategy of overbooking an office will result in a miserable situation if everyone shows up. You will then have to be very limited with your patient assessments, leaving no time to take a breather, or even have some small talk with your patients. Phoning patients to confirm a day or two before is an effective strategy to minimize no-shows.

SAMPLE 2
DAILY SCHEDULE

7:30-8:00	Set aside time for paperwork, if needed
8:00-8:30	New patient
8:30-9:00	New patient
9:00-9:30	New patient
9:30-10:00	New patient
10:00-10:15	Follow-up visit
10:15-10:30	Follow-up visit
10:30-10:45	Follow-up visit
10:45-11:00	Follow-up visit
11:00-12:00	Clinical procedure
12:00-1:00	Lunch
1:00-1:30	New patient
1:30-2:00	New patient
2:00-2:30	New patient
2:30-2:45	Follow-up visit
2:45-3:00	Follow-up visit
3:00-3:15	Follow-up visit
3:15-3:30	Follow-up visit
3:30-3:45	Follow-up visit
3:45-4:00	Follow-up visit
4:00-5:00	Review of files and results; further paperwork

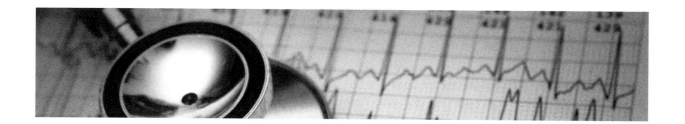

11

ANNOUNCEMENTS, PROMOTIONAL MATERIAL, AND ADVERTISING

Promoting your business is one of the more challenging and controversial areas that comes into play when setting up a medical practice. There are so many regulations, gray zones, and professionalism considerations when deciding on what extent you wish to go with for your promotion.

Be sure to research relevant guidelines and ask for advice from the appropriate authorities before getting yourself into deep water at the outset of your medical career. There are professional codes and responsibilities that you have to uphold in the medical profession as well as in the allied health professions, and each local, regional, or national authority has firm guidelines in this regard.

There are multiple modes for promotion and advertising. This chapter will describe a few methods, most being fairly standard with starting a new practice.

1. BUSINESS CARDS

Getting your new business cards is one of those exciting things that you have to do when opening your new office. Be sure to get the cards printed as far in advance of your practice opening as possible. As soon as you have all the contact details to add to your card, get them done. Basic styles of business cards are inexpensive, so if you have to reprint cards later with additional information that took a while to obtain, it is better to have cards than write details on a piece of paper, or simply ask someone to remember!

In terms of the style of business cards, there are so many different options with regard to design, innovation, quality of the material, and related costs. I personally have always tended to have a simple card with a solid, neutral color and black font, but I have seen many different styles over the years. It all depends on your own taste, and the nature of your practice. Some areas of health care lend to more creative design. Keep in mind that this is your medical practice that you are representing on your card, and some people can be influenced one way or the other by something as trivial as the look and style of your business card.

You can design the card on your own or get some help with this. Most modern computers, and certain printers, allow you to create your own business cards. You can also utilize your local printing or business store to design and print the cards for you. There are also people and companies who specialize in designing stationery and promotional material, such as graphic designers. This additional help with this process will no doubt cost you more money; however, a well-designed business card may be worth the extra expense.

There are so many different layouts you can choose for your business card, as well as how much information you want to put on it. Just remember, particularly if you are going to have older people as patients in your practice, do not make the print too small — they will not be able to read what is on it. The more information you provide on the card, the smaller the font will have to be, and many people are not interested in using reading glasses to look at a business card. Sample 3 contains different styles of business cards. I personally prefer the

SAMPLE 3
BUSINESS CARDS

Olani Bask PhD
Nutritionist

555.390.2222
www.nutritionist.bask

Dr. Steven Smith
Chiropractor

Phone: 555-333-8909
Fax: 555-333-8908
Practice Website: www.chiropractor123.com

Sandra Bob MD

Plastic & Reconstructive Surgery
Hand Surgery

123 Longer Drive
456 Shorter Avenue
South Beach North Beach

Phone: 333-333-2323
Fax: 333-333-2332

www.handssurgery@sl.com

minimalist approach, with as little on the card as needed. You can visit your local printing store, or do some surfing on the web, and find all kinds of different examples and templates for you to review.

Be to sure to remember to carry your business cards around with you at all times in the beginning stages of your practice, and while setting up. You will be surprised how fast you can give them away, often having no more cards available when asked by someone for some contact information for your new practice. Simply forgetting to take them with you on a daily basis, and having to contact people after the fact, or missing out on an opportunity, is not a good business strategy!

2. ANNOUNCEMENT CARDS

The announcement card is a mode of notification, or promotion, that is often used when someone is starting out in practice, or assuming a new position. The announcement card tells people more about you and your business.

Announcement cards can be sent out directly by you or, in my experience, forwarded by an organization or facility. It can be a bit more costly for you if you require a mass mailing, with the relevant postage and work involved.

In terms of size, the announcement card is usually larger than a business card but small enough to fit in an envelope. You might even put a photo of you on the card. Sample 4 provides two examples of announcement cards.

3. INTRODUCTORY LETTERS

Sending out introductory letters to relevant parties is practice-dependent, and not for everyone. While this is a great way of saying "hi" to people and letting them know of your business, I do believe there are a few situations where this would not be of benefit. While this might be very beneficial for a specialist who would like to get the message out to potential referring doctors, this might be less worthwhile for primary care practitioners who generally have to get the message out to a different group of people.

The tone of the letter should be friendly, effective, and definitely not too detailed or lengthy. Sample 5 is an example of how an introductory letter could be written with the intention of sending it to doctors' offices and other relevant venues. Keep in mind, while I have used the general introduction "To whom it may concern," you can also put "Dear Doctor," "Dear Health-Care Professional," or personalize these letters with specific names of people or facilities. You can also distribute a letter by email to whomever you wish.

As mentioned in Chapter 10, there are services that you might not necessarily be aware of that will help with distribution of these letters. There are professional organizations that you are affiliated with that can help you distribute your letters to the appropriate audience. I periodically receive emails from a medical association informing me of a new practice, or somebody relocating. The emails that I receive sporadically from this organization are entitled "Practice Announcement from Dr. X." I mention this primarily because I was not aware of such a service when I was involved in a start-up, and I distributed the introductory letters of my own accord.

4. FLYERS

Besides having a business card readily available, or sending out an introductory letter, utilizing flyers can further inform people of what you and your practice can offer. It might be easier to more widely disseminate flyers than letters, but they are certainly not as personal.

Announcing a **new practice** in Otolaryngology-Head and Neck Surgery / Facial Plastic Surgery

Offering general otolaryngology services as well as a broad range of procedures of the face and neck: Facelifts, eyelifts, nose jobs, facial peels, Botox, and more

Phone us today for a consultation: 555.356.4444

343 Neck Ave, Suite 143, Browtown, MO, opposite the Grand Mall

---

University of South Mountain Announcement

We are pleased to inform you that **Dr. Geoff Sines** has joined our Family Practice Unit. He did his medical training, and family practice residency, at the University of South Mountain and its affiliated regional centers.

Dr. Sines is interested in all aspects of family medicine and has a particular interest in travel medicine. He joins the other doctors at the Family Practice Unit, providing both routine and urgent care.

Geoff P. Sines, MD

Please join me in welcoming Dr. Sines to our unit.

David L. Light, Director – Family Practice Unit

INTRODUCTORY LETTER

Paula N. Flight, MD
Otolaryngology/Head and Neck Surgery
2244 Runway Crescent, Rainview
Phone: 673-555-3672 Fax: 673-555-3671

To whom it may concern:

I am pleased to inform you that as of the 15th of July 2010, I will be commencing a practice in Otolaryngology/Head and Neck Surgery.

I have recently completed my training in general otolaryngology, followed by a fellowship in facial plastic and reconstructive surgery. While my interest is specifically in nasal reconstruction, my practice is open to general ear, nose, and throat disorders of both adults and children.

I will be doing surgery at the local community facility, Rainview Regional Hospital, and I will also be able to do minor procedures in my office.

I would very much appreciate the opportunity to be involved in the care of your patients. Referrals can be faxed to the above number, or if you or your patients wish to phone directly, my staff can make the necessary arrangements.

Please feel free to contact me if you have any questions, and I look forward to being involved in the care of your patients.

Yours Sincerely,

Paula N. Flight, MD

You also have to think carefully of this as another marketing tool, but be aware that not all advertising works, and sometimes it can potentially do a disservice to you if not done well. It is best you get some professional help with designing a flyer, unless you have exceptional skills in this area! Sample 6 is an example of a flyer.

5. ADVERTISEMENTS

There are so many different venues and styles of advertising, but whatever you choose to do for advertising, make sure it is professional and tactful. A reminder that all promotional material and content, no matter what field you are in, should be professional and in keeping with guidelines outlined by your professional affiliations or licensing bodies. I cannot emphasize enough that careless, inappropriate, and tasteless promotion will not help your new practice, and could potentially get you in hot water with the public, colleagues, and related authorities.

Possible areas to advertise could include the community newspaper, regional newspaper, radio, television, or Internet. Advertising is a field in which getting help from someone experienced will help you maximize the design and the effectiveness.

SAMPLE 6
FLYER

FOREST FAMILY MEDICINE

MEDICAL CARE FOR THE ENTIRE FAMILY!

Our team of health-care professionals is enthusiastic to take care of your primary health-care needs.

Our office includes a family physician, nurse practitioner, and dietitian.

Visit our website at **forestfamilymedicine.med**
Call our office today for an appointment **845-555-2222**
4444 Care Avenue, New Blakely, SE (Free parking at the rear)

"Your well-being is our priority."

6. WEBSITE

Many physicians, or practices, have websites set up with varying degrees of complexity and innovation. Internet search engines can be a major source of exposure for such websites. There are so many options for web exposure, and many practices will hire experts in the information technology field to ensure maximum exposure, and immediate appearance during a search, particularly when certain key words are typed in the search box. This is a highly advanced and complex undertaking that can be quite costly if not well constructed and managed, so get some expert help if you wish the Internet to be an important aspect of your marketing plans.

If you browse the Internet, you will see an increasing number of websites set up for health-care practices. A website can be as simple as listing contact details and services provided, to as complex as giving details on medical conditions, links to more information, videos showing procedures, and photos of patient outcomes from medical intervention.

Some health-care professionals also encourage their patients to frequently read their websites for updates, and to contact the doctor or support staff with questions. This can eliminate unnecessary visits to the office, but something like this has to be carefully coordinated and monitored. It is a personal preference as to whether health professionals wish to engage in email communications with their patients. I know of one colleague, a pediatrician, who welcomes questions from his patients by email.

I am also familiar with a dentist who encourages communication via a website. The dentist's office also requests introductory forms to be downloaded from the website, and to be completed prior to the first visit. The office requests completed forms to be faxed or electronically submitted in advance of the visit, in case the staff have any queries about the information. The website gives patients a chance to review the billing policies, and what is covered in the practice under a dental plan. This dentist's website and the procedure provides a great way to save time on the day of the initial visit, and allows both parties to review, complete, and process the information in advance.

There is so much more information that you can provide for your patients, and prospective patients, by having an effective website. The cost for obtaining a web domain is reasonable, but you need to do some searching on the Internet to compare pricing. The most reliable and professional way to get a website up and running, and maintained, is to hire the services of a professional, or a company, who can help you with it — for a cost of course! The following list is information you should try to include on your website:

- Contact details such as address, email address, phone number, and fax number
- Hours of operation
- Information on after-hours contacts
- Map and directions to the practice
- Parking and bus routes
- Information about health-care professionals and staff
- Services offered
- Costs for services
- Forms to be completed
- References for more information
- Links to related services

- Photos
- Videos
- Testimonials
- Mission statement

7. OPEN HOUSE

You have worked so hard to get to where you are, and much preparation has gone into the setup and start of your new practice, so celebrate this! There are many different ways you can let people know that all is well and you are open for business. You will also want to show people what your new office looks like and what you have available in your office, in terms of services and equipment.

An open house is an effective way of getting people to drop in, during a set time period. Be flexible with the hours of the open house and inform as many people as you can about your event. It is also a time you can invite your family and friends to come over and see how far you have made it and what your facilities look like. There will be many people who will be proud of your accomplishments.

Food is always an appealing draw for people and might just be the deal breaker when someone is deciding on whether to actually come and visit. Depending on the time of day, the guest dynamics, your budget, and the house rules of your facility, you can also have some wine or other alcoholic drinks available for your guests. It's all about moderation, so you want to entertain and ensure that it does not turn into a rowdy party! I feel this initial outlay and extra expense can be very beneficial in the long run.

Make sure there is a lot of promotional material around, including business cards and other important information about your practice. Have your staff mingle with the guests, as these folks are the first line of contact with your practice. Make this event as informative as possible for those making the effort to attend.

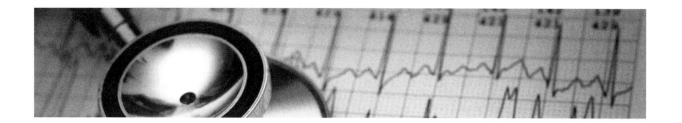

12

MAKING SURE YOUR OFFICE
RUNS SMOOTHLY

One of the most important things for a successful medical practice is to keep patients happy from the time they make that initial phone call to the moment they leave the office. Practicing exemplary medicine should always be the major factor for patient satisfaction, but often the little things count too. There are specific issues that will come into play when it comes to patient happiness. If your office is running well, then your patients will have a good experience at your practice and will therefore leave your office happy. This chapter will help you see to the little things that can help your practice run smoothly.

1. IMPORTANCE OF THE FIRST LINE OF CONTACT

The power of your first line of contact with people should never be underestimated, and this is not unique to a medical practice but rather a fact of life. Whether it be the first phone call, the recorded greeting on the phone, or that first hello from you or your staff — the first impression impacts on your prospective, or already active, patient.

Some effective briefing for your staff, positive reinforcement, and focused professional development courses can play a big role as to how well your first-line staff function. This phenomenon is relevant to all health-care professions, and I strongly encourage a supportive environment in which both your staff and patients can benefit from some active intervention and support from you.

2. AVOID LONG WAIT TIMES FOR YOUR PATIENTS

This is a topic that I have had many discussions about with my medical colleagues. I personally favor medical professionals being as on time with scheduled appointments as possible. I believe everyone's time is valuable, and wasting time in a waiting room is not beneficial for anyone. I certainly do not like to wait long periods if I am supposed to meet with a professional, no matter who he or she is. Many of us might have appointments before and after the doctor's visit, and an extended wait can impact on other plans that follow. In addition, coming to a health-care professional can be a stressful enough experience for many, and a long wait in the waiting room will not make patients feel any more comfortable with the experience. You also do not want potentially contagious patients hanging around with others for longer than is absolutely necessary.

There are some physicians who strongly believe that having a full waiting room, with some wait time, signals to the patient that the doctor is busy, successful, and thorough. It is felt that long periods of time spent with a health-care provider, and hence long wait times are synonymous with a "good" doctor. I have also heard this type of reasoning and comments on numerous occasions from patients, who indeed say how good the doctor is based on the patient volume, the full waiting room, and the associated wait time. This way of thinking applies to other aspects in life too. How many times have you walked by an empty diner, only to think that it must not be as good as the full one two doors down? Some people will even wait in a lineup for the busier restaurant, rather than going to one that does not appear to be popular, thus perpetuating a perception that it is not as good.

I am also aware of patients who do not support a chronically full waiting room, surmising that this is likely from poor office management with consistent overbooking of patients — some individuals might even decide to make alternate plans for their health care as a result of long waits.

Despite the best possible scheduling intentions, prolonged wait times are sometimes unavoidable as there can be multiple reasons as to why a health-care provider is running late. Except for the delays that are unintentional, or unavoidable, I see no benefit of poor time management in an office, resulting in perpetually long wait times for the patients in a waiting room.

3. MEDICAL RECORDS

There are several options for you as to how you wish to proceed with office documentation and records in general. I know of offices that are entirely electronic and paper free, but I am also familiar with practices that still utilize paper records for all aspects of the practice. I do have to say that the trend these days is toward the electronic world. This has benefits at multiple levels that need further mention.

Firstly, most hospitals and other health-care facilities are actively resorting to more complex and modern software that allows for easy access and utilization, both for the user and the provider. Much of what is available at these institutions is easily accessible to appropriate health-care professionals, both onsite and through distance methods. This information can be of a more general nature, or confidential information, both personal and patient related. Access can be possible from a remote computer, or some other electronic device, utilizing passwords or dedicated, secure websites. These institutional information technology systems can be complex and expensive, but for larger facilities particularly, the amount invested is a realistic option, and the benefits are immense.

In the office, everything can be set up so that your facility is paper free. There can be keyboards and monitors in all examination rooms, as well as in offices and the reception area. Many institutions and laboratories will electronically transfer all documents to your personal information technology system, alleviating any need for paper copies. This information could be laboratory results, imaging results, emergency room records, outpatient notes, and discharge summaries, to name a few sources. These can be accessed in real time while you are in the examination room with your patient. This can save an enormous amount of time and effort, trying to track down a paper copy with phone calls, faxing, etc.

In the situations in which you do receive paper copies in the mail, or from another source, there is always the opportunity to scan the documents and attach them to the electronic files. I have not heard of anyone who has made the conversion from paper to paperless complain about any possible downsides of the initiative — everyone seems happier with the ease and accessibility of the "electronic office." I have had to change some of my preferences to accommodate paperless offices of doctors who have referred patients to me. In one such situation, I chose to handwrite the consultation notes as this appeared to be the most practical way of processing the report at this specific location. It was the most efficient way to get the reports to the doctors' offices, so that they had the patient information available in the shortest possible time. It so happened that some of the offices were entirely electronic, and this handwritten note posed some challenges for them with the scan quality of the faxed note received.

If you are you going to utilize handwritten notes for whatever reason, make sure they are legible — despite doctors' infamous reputations of bad handwriting! You will hear about how damaging badly written or illegible handwritten notes can affect you should some situation arise where these notes are factored in. There are situations in which your notes can be requested, and you will be required to photocopy the file contents and forward them on. One example is a lawyer request, with signed consent from the patient. That extra effort of being more comprehensive and neat with the notes can be a major benefit to you down the road.

Of course we cannot forget sustainability, and our ongoing responsibility to the environment. If there is any way we can reduce paper use, and misuse, that should always be factored in. Having said that, I am aware of many offices that are not comfortable with a paper-free environment and we all need to do what we feel comfortable with.

4. DICTATION

While having made reference in Chapter 9 to dictation methods, this topic is worthy of further mention. Most health-care providers make use of the electronic format one way or another. Dictation is still very much a mainstay of many offices especially where a letter has to be sent to a referring doctor or other health-care provider.

While the older generation has not grown up with computers as part of their life, younger health-care professionals feel totally comfortable in front of a keyboard, and might just prefer to do the typing themselves, rather than having someone else to do it. There are few situations in which handwritten consultations and reports are used in today's technologically advanced era, electronic (i.e., dictated or typed) being the preferential method of information transfer.

As mentioned in section **3.**, I still write handwritten notes in a carbon copy format for my consultation reports at certain locations. This, however, is done in a setting where having the information immediately available is of great benefit, sometimes dictation mode being a slower process until the final result is achieved. This problem can be alleviated with new dictation technology, whereby even if the report is not typed yet, a health-care provider is able to listen to the dictation in the raw format (i.e., the voice report of the person who dictated the note). These luxuries are not available everywhere, and you have to adapt to the environment.

Dictation methods and the various formats are available in many different modes. The most traditional is a handheld, or desktop version, dictation device in which small tapes of all different shapes and sizes are used. Many offices still use this method of note taking and processing. The tape is given to the relevant office personnel for transcribing.

Another method is a built-in dictation system incorporated within the phone system of your office, or even a stand-alone system, the dictated reports being easily retrieved for processing.

Yet another method of dictating is paying an external source for typing. These services generally take care of all the processing needed, including dissemination of the report to the required destinations. This way, you phone into a distant location where you dictate your reports and their staff takes care of things for you — for a price, of course.

We cannot forget more recent voice recognition programs that automatically type things for you as you speak, but this needs some customization and fine-tuning. Often, much time is needed after to "fix up" these automated systems, so do not think that this is the ultimate solution for your own specific needs. It is a solution for some people though, but there are so many factors involved, including the quality, tone, and accent of your speaking voice.

The last thing that I need to mention is a standard template for dictation that is frequently utilized by both primary care practice and specialty offices. This way the "blanks" are filled in, particularly when repetition is common. This alleviates a bunch of unnecessary dictating and typing, where similar text, or content, is present on all reports. I have certainly used this model at different stages of my career, and for different needs. This can be for regular clinic notes, consultation notes, operating room reports, and more. While many people reading the reports might find the information repetitive from one report to the next, they generally understand that this simplifies the process and is more efficient.

There are three examples of templates to follow. Sample 7 relates to a generalist follow-up visit, Sample 8 involves a new consultation relating to a specialist, and Sample 9 relates to a surgical procedure. It is important to note that these can be designed to be only for internal use or for distribution to whomever you wish. On the CD you will find these templates, which can be modified and customized to fit just about any health-care provider. Please keep in mind that these templates would be very different depending on your area of health-care practice, but are there to give you some idea how you can customize something them for your own needs.

Sample 9 is a standard template for an example of a surgical report (inserting tubes in the eardrums). The blanks would be filled in with shortened dictation, but the transcription services would have the standard template to apply to each report. Please note that each operation can be unique, and if there is anything that does not fit in the standard template, things can be modified, or a complete dictation can be done for cases that do not fit the mold.

SAMPLE 7
FOLLOW-UP ASSESSMENT

Follow-up Assessment — Family Practice

Patient Details: _____ (already all in the office electronic system)

Date: _____

Complaint / Presenting problem / Reason for follow-up:

_____

_____

Blood Pressure: _____ Pulse: _____ Weight: _____

Progress:

_____

_____

Plan:

_____

_____

Follow-up visit: _____

Signature: _____

NEW ASSESSMENT

New Assessment – Specialist (Ear, Nose, and Throat)

Patient Details: _____ (already all in the office electronic system)

Date: _____

Presenting Complaint:
_____
_____

Past Medical History:
_____
_____

Allergies: _____ Smoking: _____ Alcohol: _____

Medications:
_____
_____

Work/Occupational History:
_____
_____

Examination

Ear:
_____

Nose:
_____

Throat:
_____

Neck:
_____

Scope:
_____

Audiology:
_____

Other investigations:
_____
_____

Summary/Diagnosis:

_____

_____

Follow-up plan (if needed): _____

Signature: _____

5. INVESTIGATIONS AND RESULTS

Investigations and results are such an important part of your practice — I cannot stress enough that you should be extremely diligent with this process. Firstly, it is crucial for your patients that all records are reviewed in a timely fashion. Being negligent with review of results can have disastrous effects on your patients.

In addition to the potential adverse outcome for patients, it can be a legal nightmare for you. A doctor will have no legs to stand on for missing or ignoring abnormal results and the ramifications can be severe. It is the doctor's office's responsibility to appropriately follow up on all abnormal results, and ultimately you, as the attending health-care provider, are the most responsible person and will have to be accountable.

Many patients are afraid of abnormal results being missed and will contact the office no matter what, but by far the majority will leave the onus on you and your office to which they have entrusted their care to let them know if something needs follow-up.

What can you do to make sure no problems arise when ordering investigations, and subsequently reviewing the results?

1. For paper reports, make sure all relevant sources have your correct mailing address, phone number, fax number, and possibly email address.

2. Your office needs to have systems in place so that the most accurate, and appropriate, contact details of patients are available and in your office at all times. Your staff, if possible, should confirm contact information with each subsequent visit.

3. Sign off on all results before they get filed. If you have paper copies, sign each and every result that comes in — for most practices this is totally doable, for others this could be practically impossible, but some safe follow-up system needs to be in place. For a paperless office, ensure that there is a plan in place whereby you can electronically sign off on results.

STANDARD TEMPLATE FOR SURGICAL REPORT

Patient Details: _____

Date: _____

Preoperative Diagnosis:
_____

Postoperative Diagnosis:
_____

Procedure
Bilateral Myringotomy and Tubes:
_____

Surgeon:
_____

Assistant:
_____

History:
_____

Procedure:

- The patient entered the room and was anesthetized using mask anesthesia. An intravenous line was also inserted.

- Starting with the right side, the tympanic membrane was well visualized utilizing the microscope and an ear speculum.

- An anterior-inferior incision was made in the tympanic membrane using the myringotomy blade. Fluid was suctioned from the middle ear.

- A short beveled tube was inserted into the tympanic membrane *(standard make of tube that you commonly use would be inserted here as part of the template)*.

- In a similar fashion, a myringotomy and tube insertion was performed on the left side.

- The patient was awoken from the anesthetic and returned to the recovery room in a satisfactory condition.

- The procedure occurred uneventfully, and no complications were encountered.

4. Make sure abnormal results are flagged for your staff. The patient's files, or relevant information, will then have to be retrieved and the necessary action taken. It could mean a phone call, a follow-up visit, or a referral to another health-care provider.

5. For abnormal results, as a back-up, make a notation, or keep a log, to make sure things do not get misplaced somewhere in the tracking phase. Every week look at your list to make sure you have covered the issue at hand. For those doctors who have large volumes of abnormal results (e.g., numerous blood tests), maybe the significantly abnormal ones can be additionally kept on lists, on top of the normal flagging system that you have in place.

6. For results that come to you electronically, make sure there is a process whereby you can flag them and apply the same tracking system as on the paper copies.

7. For some doctors, there could be multiple sources in which results may arrive, such as by regular mail, fax, or a hospital mailbox. I have always tried to make sure my results all come to one source. It might mean more effort and cost to yourself and others, but I think this is the safest way to be comprehensive and timely with reviews. The more places you have where results can arrive, the more potential for error.

8. One extra safety barrier, which I have utilized in some offices in which I have worked, particularly when it is on an irregular basis, is a proactive tracking sheet. When investigations are ordered they are tabulated on a spreadsheet for easy reference. The list can be reviewed periodically for progress of the

investigation. This method has worked well in some cases where somehow a test, or procedure, has fallen through the cracks, which is something you want to avoid at all costs.

There can be many reasons for a planned investigation not proceeding, such as a change of address, a no-show, or a fax being misplaced. Once again it has to be emphasized that not all practices can monitor something like this with such rigor, particularly where the amount of tests being ordered are excessive. Whatever you do, make sure abnormal tests are picked up and followed up on.

It might be a good idea to post a list in the reception area such as the one in Sample 10. Naturally, this list can be modified to meet your own needs. Note that this form is on the CD under the file name Efficient Management of Investigations, available for you to modify.

6. EMERGENCY PROVISIONS

Each type of practice will have a unique requirement as to what you need to have available in the office in case of unexpected emergencies. Often this will also be dictated by standard practice guidelines and standards of care, as mandated by local or national regulating bodies. Be vigilant in checking with licensing authorities, medical societies, and other relevant parties as to what is required in an office or practice like yours.

Such requirements could include oxygen, airway management equipment (e.g., ventilation equipment), intravenous supplies, emergency medications, and more. While emergency situations might not happen very often in a primary care practice, or many specialty offices, do not be caught off guard. Besides the obvious benefits for the patient and the act of saving someone's life, you could find yourself in trouble with the authorities for not being adequately equipped in your medical office.

I can remember one specific situation in which an elderly gentleman collapsed in the examination chair while I was performing a minor procedure. Had it not been for emergency equipment, which had not been used for years but acquired at the time I set up the practice, the outcome could have been fatal. I was able to do what I could to keep the patient stable in the office setting before emergency services arrived. Just a reminder: It is important to periodically check expiry dates on all relevant equipment so that it can be replaced if necessary.

In addition to guidelines or expectations as mentioned earlier, there might be situations in which you have no choice in the matter if you want to practice, depending on what type of office you have. For certain practices where you could be performing procedures with some risk, there might be accreditation procedures whereby your office has to meet predetermined standards of care. You could require an evaluation by an external body to see if you meet requirements. If you fail to comply on an ongoing basis with such regulations, your office could be shut down, in addition to the possible consequences for your future eligibility to practice in such a setup.

SAMPLE 10
EFFICIENT MANAGEMENT OF INVESTIGATIONS LIST FOR OFFICE STAFF

1. Accurate office contact details on all requisitions.

2. Make sure patient details are accurate and up-to-date.

3. Make sure investigations are filled out completely.

4. Timely review of all incoming results.

5. Responsible health-care provider (or appropriate delegate) to sign off on all returning results.

6. Flag all abnormal results.

7. Retrieve file or relevant information relating to flagged result.

8. Contact patients with abnormal results. Schedule follow-up visit if necessary.

9. Consider tracking system to ensure receipt of results.

10. Attempt to arrange that all mail comes to one address.

11. Timely checking of additional mail locations (e.g., hospital mail box).

Sample 11 is an example of an emergency provisions checklist (which should be reviewed on a regular basis). Please note that this list would have to be considerably modified depending on your type of health-care profession.

7. AFTER-HOURS COVERAGE

After-hour commitments vary significantly from one health-care provider to the next. Some health-care professionals might have to be, or wish to be, always available for contact. This might be directly from patients or from a health-care facility, or from both. On the other extreme, some medical professionals will, by choice, not take on any after-hours commitments at all, and essentially have practices that function without the need for being on-call. There are some specialties in which being on-call is not usually a requirement or need. An example of such a clinical domain is developmental pediatrics, where usually no emergency coverage is necessary. There are other clinical areas in which being on-call is synonymous with the job; a general surgeon and a general pediatrician are a couple examples.

Whatever your situation may be, make sure adequate provisions are in place for your practice when you are not physically in the office. This could take on many forms — some examples are voice mail giving adequate instructions, a message providing contact information for alternate coverage, your phone calls forwarded elsewhere, or a third party taking the calls on your behalf. The scope of coverage is so varied for providing this after-hours, or so-called on-call service. Let's give you an example of two family physicians and how this very point can be so different.

Dr. Hans is a general practitioner in a small town, quite far away from a large medical center. She chooses to always be available for her patients after hours, should the need arise. Dr. Hans provides a contact phone number, as well as a pager number, for her patients to contact her at any time. Her patients seem to be aware as to when to go directly to the small local hospital, wait until the next day, or contact Dr. Hans after hours. Patients rarely call Dr. Hans after hours.

Dr. Mull is a family physician in a solo practice located in a suburban area of a large city. His office is generally open from nine to five, and closed on the weekends. Dr. Mull has chosen an after-hours service to cover his patients' calls outside of his office hours. His phone is automatically rerouted to this company's switchboard. This organization is made of a group of physicians who share a roster to provide after-hours coverage for primary care physicians who wish to contract such a service.

Whatever your choice for after office hours, it a very important area to ensure appropriate and accurate information is provided to your patients. This could even be the difference between a life and death situation; for example, a person may need adequate direction for dealing with a potential emergency.

Do not leave patients in the lurch when they are trying to get hold of you. You are not obliged to be available at all times, but alternative plans must be clear for your patients, something even as simple as a short informative voice message. Of course, there are those situations in which you have to be on-call, when on a hospital roster for example, unless you find a colleague to do it for you. For the most part, after-hours coverage is part of the territory for health-care professionals.

MEDICAL OFFICE EMERGENCY PROVISIONS CHECKLIST

1. Instructions in the event of a medical emergency in each examination room, one in the reception area, and one in each doctor's office.

2. Mask and bag set-up for the airway.

3. Airway tubes (relevant to the skill of the office medical professionals and staff).

4. Suction setup.

5. Oxygen supply.

6. Intravenous cannulae.

7. Intravenous tubing and fluids.

8. Skin cleaning materials and necessary adhesives.

9. Emergency medications.

10. List of relevant emergency numbers in all rooms.

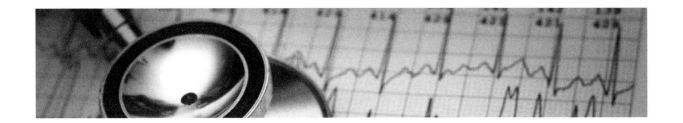

13

ADDITIONAL TOPICS TO CONSIDER

As you are setting up your practice you will have many things to consider. This chapter discusses some things you may have overlooked in your initial setup plans.

1. OFFICE HOURS

Everyone has their own style and preferences when it comes to office hours. Some offices prefer to make it clear at all times as to exact opening and closing times. Others prefer to be flexible as to what information is shared with patients regarding office hours. It mostly depends what type of practice you have, and there are so many variables. It is often easier for patients if you have set hours.

Your phone message can be changed daily, which is what many offices do. Alternatively, you can have a general message, which does

not allude to precise office hours, thus avoiding having to change the message daily. For those practices where the hours and schedule can vary from day to day, having a general message is often the preferred route.

Whatever you decide on in terms of providing the relevant information for your patients, be sure to always keep your office staff's safety in mind, especially when a possibility might arise of patients arriving to an office where only one staff member is on hand.

In my practice, my medical office assistant always kept the door closed and locked when she was alone, unless there was an expected visit from someone. There were a couple of compromising situations that she found herself in, and that prompted us to keep things closed up when nobody else was around. It is always better to be safe than sorry. That is an example of where you learn new things as you go along with a new office setup, and there is no cookie-cutter approach for every office.

2. CHILD SAFETY

Unless you have a practice limited to infants and children, this is something that might not be on the radar screen when you are planning things. Just like any home where there are small children running around, you are obliged to make sure your office is childproof. There are many things in a doctor's office that can be fatal when discovered, or consumed, by a roaming and inquisitive child.

The most obvious thing to immediately take care of before you open your doors for the first time is to remove all toxic materials and substances from reach of children, and make sure there is a safety lock on any cupboard door that is accessible to small children. Also avoid keeping any unnecessary toxic solutions or materials in your office that are not absolutely needed. Often things just hang around from a previous practice for no reason, so remove anything you don't need. If you do need potentially toxic products, be very vigilant with storage.

An important factor in terms of child safety, which is often overlooked, is the nature of any toys that you might have in your office for child use. Choking hazards from inappropriate toys in a doctor's office is inexcusable. Examine each toy carefully and watch for new toys that just arrive and remain in your waiting room or examination rooms. Not uncommonly, patients leave toys unintentionally, or even intentionally as a goodwill gesture. I can recall several situations in which patients donated toys for my waiting room, only for me to discard some of them due to safety concerns.

While on the topic of toys, here are some more points that I think are worthy of further mention. Avoid purchasing any toys that are noisy when used by children because they will irritate your adult patients in the waiting room. They will also be a distraction for your office staff if they are in close range of the children's play area. I can remember a push toy lawnmower that drove everyone around the bend, so this toy did not last long in the waiting room.

Also, if you are going to have books in the office, screen them first as to whether they are appropriate for your young patients. You will be surprised as to the content of some children's books. I certainly was, and will always remember a mom bringing to my attention some content of one of the books in the waiting room. It was supposed to be a text intended for young children, but it was rather violent in nature both relating to story content and writing style. Since that time, I screen all books that are for use in my office before the patients see them. This was definitely not on my to-do list at the outset, but I soon learned!

Another factor that is on the forefront of many of our minds is the transmission of bugs through contact, and children's toys are no exception to germs. While this is a challenging task to take into consideration, there are some things you can do to lessen the risk. Keep away from toys that are not easy to keep clean, such as stuffed animals. Toys should also be cleaned periodically.

3. READING MATERIAL

Besides the books mentioned in section **2.** for children, most offices have some materials available for general reading. These can be books, magazines, and newspapers. It is always nice to have at least one daily newspaper for your patients to read. There are all kinds of special deals for professional offices for newspaper and magazine subscriptions, so make sure you make use of these opportunities.

No matter who the audience is in your waiting room, make sure the content is appropriate for your patient population. Also, review the reading material laying around in your waiting room every now and again as you will be surprised what patients accidentally and deliberately leave in your office. I have often removed religious material that was clearly left with intention, and totally inappropriate for inclusion in the pile of reading material for patients.

It is astonishing to see, at several offices that I have worked at, the amount of outdated reading material, sometimes up to five years old. I feel very strongly that you can spend a little money keeping your office current in all aspects, including material for your patients to keep themselves occupied with while waiting to see you.

Just like with children's toys, there is always the possibility of cold and flu viruses being transmitted with shared magazines and other reading materials. After the recent outbreak of the H1N1 virus, some offices have done away with providing reading materials at all.

4. OTHER NICE THINGS TO HAVE IN THE WAITING ROOM

The sky is the limit as to what you wish to have in your waiting room. Many offices will have a filtered water dispenser for patient use, while others might have coffee or tea, too. Some might go even further by providing snacks or complimentary telephone and computer use. These latter luxuries I have tended to see

more in professional offices where competition for patient business is a big factor. I have certainly seen cosmetic surgeons' and dentists' offices that look like a five-star hotel lobby or a business lounge!

Keep in mind that some of the things that you might want in a waiting room might not be such a wise idea. Take for example live plants; while they look nice and are certainly more authentic than fake plants, patients with environmental allergies might not be so thrilled. This is particularly important when your patient population in a certain specialty might be comprised of more people with allergy problems. My advice is to keep away from plants, flowers, or any other allergenic, nice things to have. There are other ways to make your office look attractive without potentially making your patients sicker!

5. RETENTION OF FILES

You just never know when you might make a change, or something untoward can happen. Just like with disability or life insurance, you need to plan for unforeseen circumstances in the future. Depending on the jurisdiction where you practice, there are guidelines about how long you are required to store or retain files. There are minimum time periods you need to keep files that are stipulated by the relevant authorities, and not planning ahead for this can have a significant impact on your office space.

Two offices that I have been affiliated with did not make provisions early on in the office setup for adequate file storage, due to minimum required retention time. This required innovative ways to keep up with the ever-increasing number of patient files and associated storage space. One office required a redesign of the file storage area with sliding filing cabinets, and the other situation involved extending the storage area to the ceiling of the office, thus having to use a stepladder on a frequent basis. It is easy to store older files off-site, such as in your home or elsewhere, but it can be quite inconvenient when reviewing patients that you saw several years back and now need to check the old records for information.

These challenges further support the notion of a paper-free, or electronic, office. The amount of space saved when you don't have to consider paper file storage is significant, needless to say so is the extra money you would be paying per square foot of storage space. A paper-free office would also help with your contribution to sustainability of the environment.

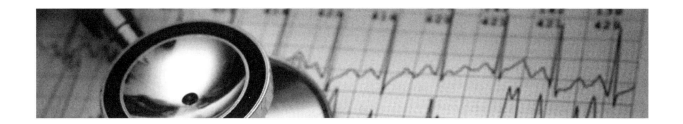

14

BILLING OF SERVICES

Money is often a topic that seems to be synonymous with doctors. Money should never be the motivating factor for doing medicine. Doctors get remunerated in so many different ways, which differ immensely across the globe, as well as within specific geographic regions. Many doctors starting up in practice might not be so savvy with the money side of things, but need to learn quickly so the office can function efficiently in all aspects from the beginning. This is not something that is readily discussed with prospective medical students, or adequately covered with residents, but it is important that this piece of the puzzle is included in the big picture. No matter which health-care profession you are committing yourself to, the money side of things will come into play at one point or another.

As for the specific amounts that doctors and other health-care providers earn, there is immense variability depending on many factors. All you need to do is be a bit innovative with your Google searches and you will find all the information you need. Do not spend too much time getting wrapped up in this though. Rather than give you all the different scenarios and variables, I will illustrate a few ways in which doctors, and other health-care providers, can get paid. Those about to set up an office might know all of this already, but others might not be aware of such things.

Note that billing practices are quite similar between the different health-care professions, although there can be significant differences as to what is all covered in different health-care plans.

Example 1

Dr. Heed is an orthopedic surgeon and works with a Health Maintenance Organization (HMO) in California. The way an HMO works is that it provides care to patients only by physicians who are contracted by the organization. Dr. Heed has agreed to work for the HMO and comes into this setup with a steady stream of patient referrals already in place within the HMO system.

Dr. Heed decided to join an HMO as she did not want to go through the challenges of starting a practice on her own. Starting her own practice would entail, amongst other things, working hard at getting a patient-referral basis set up. (Depending on the location a person chooses to practice, this can be a hard task, especially if supply outweighs demand.) Dr. Heed also likes the financial remuneration method whereby she has chosen to receive a fixed salary per month, irrespective of the amount of patients seen. There are some incentives and bonuses involved with this payment setup, but for the most part she receives a standard amount each month. Many doctors prefer this method of payment, while others prefer to receive money for whatever they do (fee-for-service).

Example 2

Dr. Ols is a family physician in a busy community practice in rural Canada. He sees patients in a manner whereby he charges for services based on a fee scedule, known to many as fee-for-service billing. In Canada, with the national health-care system, the majority of doctors bill the provincial governments for services provided. Dr. Ols refers to standard billing codes and fee structures, which are standard for the province in which he works, in order to process the billings. He receives payments on a bimonthly basis from the provincial billing agency with detailed reconciliation information. Sometimes, there can even be helpful statistical information that can give Dr. Ols an idea as to how his billing numbers, or practices, compare with those of his colleagues who are in a similar practice profile.

Example 3

Dr. Lind is a cosmetic surgeon who works on Harley Street in London, England. She works mostly in private practice, although she has some education commitments, providing continuing medical education for practicing doctors.

Many health-care professionals who work in this situation also work in the National Health Service (NHS) and are attached to teaching hospitals. While the NHS provides the majority of health care in the United Kingdom, there are doctors who prefer to work in the private sector.

Dr. Lind bills her patients directly for services rendered. As payment methods, her office accepts cash, checks, all major credit cards, interbank transfers, and even flexible financing options. She has primarily chosen this method of practice, as she prefers to work independently from the national health-care system. She also likes to be her own boss and prefers to decide how things are run in her practice, and not be ruled by government or other funding plans.

Example 4

Dr. Nisk is an internal medicine specialist in a big city in North America. He enjoys diversity in terms of the ways he chooses to practice medicine. He has his own office in close proximity to the local hospital, he sees patients at this hospital, and is periodically on-call for the emergency department and inpatient wards. He also has an appointment with the local university, which is in the downtown area, where he teaches medical students and residents on a regular basis.

Dr. Nisk's income comes from different sources. He receives his fee-for-service billing from the health-related authority, on-call stipend from the same authority (through the hospital billing system), and then gets some teaching money from the university. He also does research, which he really enjoys, but he receives no money from that — just a lot of gratification.

Example 5

Dr. Sel is a dentist in a big urban center. While there are different options for her to bill patients for dental services, Dr. Sel has decided to bill patients directly for amounts owing, and this needs to be completed on the same day, just after the visit is completed. If the patient has dental coverage, he or she will get a reimbursement directly from his or her insurance company after that time. It will likely be a lesser amount than the payment, as Dr. Sel has opted to charge patients 20 percent more than the maximum fee reimbursement by most companies. For some patients this process will be expedited by a direct submission for reimbursement through the dentist's office; for others, they might have to mail proof of payment to the insurance company.

Example 6

Dr. Duy is a chiropractor who works in a multi-specialty clinic in a community setting. He is responsible for his own billing and then pays a monthly fee to the facility for the space and services. His charges are above the amount permitted by the local provincial health-insurance plan. Dr. Duy chooses to bill the patient at the time of the visit, but only the amount that is beyond what will be paid through the provincial health plan. The patient can then submit this additional amount paid to a supplementary health-insurance plan, which covers this portion of the payment. In addition, once a threshold has been reached for chiropractic services permitted by the provincial plan, the patient will be responsible for the subsequent visits, which in turn may be covered by a supplementary health plan.

1. BILLING PRACTICES

There are many ways you can earn your money as a health-care professional. The opportunities are immense, and your billing preferences are often something that you can choose.

I have worked in many different environments, involving a variety of payment options, each with its own benefits and downsides. Sometimes you will have a choice as to the method of payment, other times you will have to fit in with what is already in place. It is always wise to cover options for a potential increase in salary and other incentives before you commit to a position. While, for example, a 50/50 income split with a facility where you are working might seem reasonable at the outset, with time you may realize that it should be more like 60/40. If you do not adequately explore all options before you start, it could be difficult to amend down the road.

It should be mentioned that there are countries in the world and situations where there is no choice as to how you receive your earnings because your practice will be exclusively funded by the government or other institutional bodies.

1.1 Fee-for-service

In fee-for-service you bill either the patient or a third party for services rendered. This third party might be an insurance company, provincial health-care plan, law-enforcement organization, or military body. The amount is related more to actual services rendered, versus a block of time or services.

Depending on whom or what you are billing, you might have a time limit for submitting a bill, three months for example. You also might provide a stipulated time to a patient in which the bill has to be paid without additional charge. These types of time limits are often quite variable, mostly depending on the individual circumstances.

Many health providers will also send a reminder notice for an outstanding bill, but remember that these initiatives require time and manpower, something that you will have to pay more for. Particularly in the case of insurance companies being the main source of a health provider's fees, an enormous amount of rigor and tracking will have to take place in order to be paid for the services rendered.

Whatever your setup is, if you have to submit invoices or fees, make sure you are fully aware from the outset as to any time limitations for submission and processing of these amounts.

1.2 Salary

You receive a set amount per annum or per month when it comes to salary. There might be a flexible setup associated whereby you receive a bonus beyond a certain threshold of billings accrued (the base salary being the threshold over which further percentage billings are accrued). Payments could be monthly, bimonthly, or by some other arrangement.

Benefits might also be included; medical, dental, disability and life insurance, and pension plans are some examples.

1.3 Contractual

Contractual billing can take on many forms, but usually involves some predetermined amount of work, or set rate, for a service provided. An example of this might be providing services for a correctional institution, taking approximately one day per workweek, for a three-year period. You are provided with a set income that is not dependent on exactly how much time you spend there, or how many patients you see, but rather based on a time commitment.

Another example might be a three-month task in an educational setting, in which you have been asked to be involved with some initiative that requires your expertise.

1.4 Income splitting and commission

I prefer to use the term income splitting rather than commission. In this situation, the healthcare professional works in an environment where he or she gives a portion of the earnings to the employer, or the employer gives part of the income to the provider. On many occasions, the other party you are dealing with is a fellow colleague. In other situations, this might be the owner of the establishment, who is not a clinician himself or herself.

Such an arrangement might be a 50/50 or 60/40 split, or whatever is mutually arranged. The percentage split is often determined by what overhead and services the employer provides. This is also directly associated with what field you are in as some offices might have minimal expenses. The lower the office overhead and other running costs of the practice, the better your piece of the pie should be. If you are in this category of remuneration, be resourceful and do all your research before committing to a certain amount.

1.5 Associate or locum tenens arrangements

As mentioned in Chapter 4, associate or locum tenens arrangements can take on many forms, but generally they involve working in someone else's office, usually an already established practice. You could have either a fixed arrangement of working full-time, part-time, or even sporadically. Some commitments might be long term; others might be short term, covering for a sick leave, maternity or paternity absence, or even helping out when the volume of work increases in the office. The actual manner in which the you get paid can be quite variable and can involve any of the funding methods discussed, including salary, fee-for-service, or income splitting arrangements.

1.6 Block payments

There are some jurisdictions and organizations globally that compensate you based on a specific group or number of patients. This is not uncommon in the British medical system, or in North America for that matter. Depending on your personal preferences, many health-care providers favor a system like this, as you can concentrate on the task at hand and not be preoccupied by the number of patients you have to see per day to cover your expenses and for an adequate income.

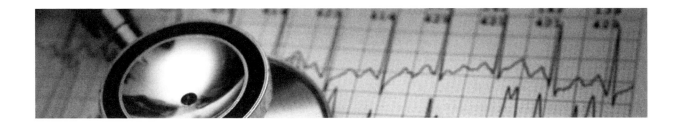

15

EVALUATING YOUR PRACTICE

Once you have your practice up and running, you will need to evaluate how you and your staff are doing to make sure you are on the right track. This chapter will cover some of the things you will need to consider.

1. DIRECT FEEDBACK

There is no better way to find out how you are doing with your new practice than to find out directly from the patients themselves. Direct feedback can be obtained from casual conversations, a comment box, or even a short survey. You can also solicit comments while with your patients, or your staff can ask the patients directly about their experience in your office. I have often asked patients how they have found the experience in the office, or about specific situations such as wait times or efficiency and ease of the office.

Be sure to always pass on the good comments to the relevant people, especially if they are not present at the time. Also provide some constructive and supportive feedback for any negative comments you might receive. It is important to weigh the context of the negative comments made before making an issue of them — sometimes it might involve some investigation so you have all your bases covered.

Sample 12, which is also included on the CD, provides you with a short patient survey. You might consider utilizing something like this.

SURVEY FOR PATIENTS

1. How did you find the pre-appointment arrangements with our office?

Good: _____ Satisfactory: _____ Needs improvement: _____

Comments:

_____

2. How were you received on arrival at the office?

Good: _____ Satisfactory: _____ Needs improvement: _____

Comments:

_____

3. How was your wait time before being seen by the doctor?

Good: _____ Satisfactory: _____ Needs improvement: _____

Comments:

_____

4. How would you rate your experience with the doctor?

Good: _____ Satisfactory: _____ Needs improvement: _____

Comments:

_____

6. How did you find the exit instructions and follow-up plans (if needed)?

Good: _____ Satisfactory: _____ Needs improvement: _____

Comments:

_____

7. What was your overall impression of your visit to our office today?

Good: _____ Satisfactory: _____ Needs improvement: _____

Comments:

_____

2. INDIRECT FEEDBACK

Whether you like it or not, people are going to make comments about you and your practice, which you are going to hear about through someone else. Hopefully the comments are positive, but in reality if a patient has had a bad experience, he or she is more likely to speak about it than if he or she had a good experience, and the story can be very one-sided.

While it is human nature to be sensitive to these negative comments, and take things personally, many times criticism can be constructive. Things to improve in your practice that might be lacking or suboptimal can be pointed out. Do not get too bent out of shape if you hear something negative about your office, but rather use the information as a tool to improve things.

I can think of several situations in which taking comments has allowed me to use the information in a positive sense. Naturally if I hear something good about my staff, or the work they are doing, I will always pass this information on to them. In my mind there is very little that beats positive reinforcement in the work setting.

One negative comment that comes to mind is someone who once told me he always seemed to have difficulty faxing information due to a continually busy signal on our end. With that came the implication that it is difficult to refer patients to my office. It so happened that the assistant at the time was faxing a lot of reports during the day that and that caused a constantly busy line. We made a plan to do our faxing mostly early in the morning and at the end of the day. This allowed for longer periods of free time on the fax machine, which sorted out the problem that caused the comment to come my way. At a later time, we purchased a more advanced fax machine that allowed for storing of multiple faxes at the same time. This is just one example of how negative commentary can help you improve on an area in your practice.

Whether you like it or not, there are numerous other venues where the public can rate your performance for the world to see. If you do an Internet search on any health-care provider, you are bound to find all kinds of information for your perusal. Some of these comments can be quite constructive, while others might be disturbing for a health-care provider to read. While I would imagine most comments are sincere, and there to help the public with choosing a doctor, other postings might be there to bear a grudge or for another obscure reason. You need to be aware of these sites, but how you wish to read and interpret them will be left in your hands. Some doctors check on these sites frequently to assess the status of their ratings, while other doctors ignore them. There are some examples of these websites in the Resources section on the CD.

3. PERIODIC REVIEW

A periodic review is an exercise that I highly recommend be done on a yearly basis, this being an effective method of quality control. There are so many different ways you can do this, ranging from the most informal format to a very structured process. The bottom line is that you want to make sure you are running things in the office the best you can. This can be by looking at things closely from an operational standpoint, a medical practice review, or a combination of both. It is best you do this yourself, before something like this is imposed on you by a third party for whatever reason.

In its simplest form, you could get your staff together and talk about the strengths and weaknesses of the office, or address patient comments, questions, and concerns. On the other end of the spectrum, you could have a document that you have developed which methodically covers all the important aspects of your office.

4. SELF-ASSESSMENT TOOLS

There is so much available these days in terms of self-assessment tools, mostly relating to practice review. These resources can be educational as well as give you an ability to review your practice and clinical skills in a safe environment. You can do this when and where it's convenient for you and at your own pace.

Many self-assessment tools are also considered continuing education, and this way the hours spent can be logged as self-study, if indeed you are required by authorities to report continuing medical education. Be sure to check all the necessary sources with the organizations associated with your specialty so that you are fully aware of what's available for you. The Resources section on the CD includes some examples of online resources related to self-assessment.

5. LECTURES AND ROUNDS

No matter what type of health-care professional you are, there are educational lectures, rounds, and other similar venues for you to keep up-to-date. Lectures and rounds also help you to stay connected with your colleagues and peers. The quality and make-up of these educational sessions vary immensely.

Technological advancements have enabled distance attendance, both in real time and at a later date. Examples include videoconferencing, teleconferencing, and podcasting. Just take a look at any website for a medical school and you will find information relating to lectures and rounds. By attending, or reviewing, these educational sessions, you have the opportunity to evaluate how you are practicing in your health-care profession, while learning new things. The Resources section on the CD includes links to educational information.

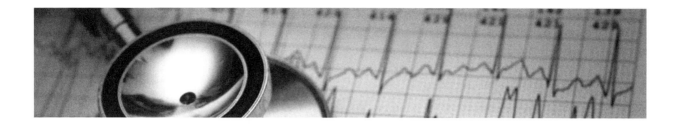

16

TROUBLESHOOTING

While we always hope for a smooth and uncomplicated day in the office, there are situations that catch us off guard. Being aware and prepared is half the battle in terms of sorting out troublesome situations, or at least understanding them. There are many situations that each of us who have been in a practice can talk about, and several parts of this book could be repeated in a modified form in this section, but I have highlighted a few about which I think you, and your staff, should have some idea. It might be a good idea to keep a document for your office staff to refer to, as so much of this problem solving can be done by someone other than the heath-care provider. (See Checklist 6 at the end of this chapter.)

1. WHAT TO DO WHEN A STAFF MEMBER PHONES IN SICK

Employees will get sick in an office setting at one point or another. There are so many different solutions that can be utilized in this type of situation. Of course, this is easier to deal with when there is more than one employee. The following scenarios will help you troubleshoot this type of problem.

1.1 Family or friends cover the shift

You might have a family member, friend, or someone else close to you who can step in at short notice. If possible, it is always prudent to have an individual who is not a regular employee in the office to know the basics of your office for any emergency situation. There are many office settings where a family member who is familiar with the office, can help out and keep apprised of the goings on.

I am also aware of many offices where a spouse is closely involved in the day-to-day running of the office. This situation is obviously very dependent on the people and whether a setup like this can work for you, without this being a cause for the end of a marriage or relationship is up to you! For more information see Chapter 9.

1.2 Everyone in the office pitches in

Another option is to make do with what you have and work around it. If you have other staff, everyone can pitch in to cover for the absent employee to get the job done. Obviously, much modification would be needed to compensate for the absent person, but I have generally found patients to be understanding and supportive when unexpected events like this arise.

If you have only one staff member, it's obviously more challenging, but I have seen offices run in this situation. This scenario includes a doctor running the office himself or herself in the event that the only other employee calls in sick at the last minute. This is a good reason why it's best for the employee to get everything ready for the following day before he or she leaves — you just never know when this preparation might come in handy.

1.3 Contact temporary staffing agencies

Depending on your location of practice there are temporary staffing agencies that can be utilized at the last minute. These businesses specialize in providing office services for unplanned absences, as well as for absences that are known in advance.

Staffing agencies can be of benefit if there is a particular time that you need some extra temporary help. I have certainly made use of these services on a periodic basis when the need has arisen, due to illness or vacation of staff. It can be quite costly, and the skill set of the temporary staff variable, but it is most valuable in unforeseen situations.

1.4 Close until employee returns

The last option is to close shop until things can get sorted out. This last resort is not something that I have seen occur very often, but if functioning of an office is dependent on having an assistant, then this is might be your only option.

In the event of this unfortunate situation, patients should be notified of the change, and voice-mail messages should be modified. The appointments will need rescheduling, making for a busy time when the office opens again.

2. SAFETY ISSUES WHILE WITH A PATIENT

Difficult and potentially unsafe situations can occur when you least expect them. They can occur when you are seeing a patient for the first time, or even with follow-up visits. You have no idea how patients are going to respond to certain questions during your history taking, examinations needing to be performed, discussion of diagnoses, or while covering the management plan.

If you feel a compromising situation starting to develop for yourself, rather than let the situation escalate, excuse yourself from the room for a moment. Take a few deep breaths, reflect on what has just occurred, and consider your next steps. If you sense immediate danger, phone emergency services for help, or security if you have that option onsite. If you are uncertain about how to handle the situation, make a quick phone call to whomever you feel comfortable talking to and get some advice.

It's important to alert your staff about what to do in a situation like this. Most importantly, your staff needs to know when to call for help. My experience with these types of encounters is to avoid escalation of anger and tempers at all costs. Just like fire drill protocols, it might be useful for you to outline strategies with your staff before problems occur.

Having a panic button is always a good idea, which can be used both in the event of a medical emergency in the office or an unsafe situation. I would like to emphasize that you or your staff being in danger is an exceptionally rare occurrence, but certain types of patient dynamics, or the nature of your clinical practice, can make this more common for some.

In the event of a situation like this and after all is quiet, it is wise to sit down with others in your office to debrief by going over the situation. Was there anything that could have been done better? Is there a plan that can come out of this if a similar situation arises in the future?

The following are some ideas to summarize how to deal with a difficult patient situation:

1. If anyone is at risk for harm, call 911 and in-house security immediately, as would be the case in any other risky situation.

2. If a conversation or situation looks like it is going down the wrong path, leave the room, gather your thoughts and composure, and decide on your next steps.

3. It is appropriate to ask a patient who is acting inappropriately to leave the office. If it looks like that might inflame the situation more, call 911 or in-house security.

4. If you are able to sort out the situation yourself, you then have to decide if you wish to see the patient again. Contact your local medical licensing authorities — they will be able to give you guidance as to how the termination of a patient-doctor relationship can be carried out.

Ending a doctor-patient relationship can be a very difficult decision, but something you sometimes have to do. Be sure to explore all your options and seek professional guidance before you carry out something like this. Very often there are structured guidelines from your professional associations that will help you through this, including providing template documents for you.

3. MANAGEMENT IN THE EVENT OF A FIRE ALARM

There should be standard measures and procedures for any facility when it comes to a fire alarm and evacuation. Some buildings have better instructions than others, and evacuation routes vary immensely from one building to the next. Be sure you and your office staff are familiar with fire drills and procedures. If it is not clearly outlined in your office, or orientation is not provided by the building management, seek clarification.

Whatever environment you are in, abide by the plan that is in place for your office building in the event of a fire alarm. There are situations that are unforeseeable such as being in the middle of a procedure on a patient and sudden evacuation is required. While there is no specific answer for all in these types of scenarios, I strongly encourage you to consult with your local acute-health-care facility for input as to how it handles these challenges. Evacuation should be handled similarly to how a fire alarm in an operating room environment when patients are anesthetized and in the middle of the procedure would be.

4. PROLONGED PATIENT VISIT

While you can try your best to book patients in adequate time intervals, periodically you will have a situation in which a patient visit far exceeds the allocated time. There are many reasons for this, including a complex medical problem, an unplanned procedure, language barrier, or a longer than expected discussion. It's better to spend longer with the patient in an attempt to understand or resolve the situation, than rush things through.

There are several ways of dealing with this. Also, you have to weigh the implications from running significantly late, both for your schedule and those of the patients following the visit. While patient safety always comes first (and there is no negotiation in that department), my advice is to do whatever it takes to keep calm in your office, particularly keep yourself calm — you do not want to be seeing patients while stressed out.

Possibilities for resolution of prolonged visits include asking the patient to return another time to complete the visit, allowing your patient the opportunity to sit in the waiting room while you see some other patients first, referring to another physician if clinically indicated, or just spending that extra time and dealing with the consequences that might occur. Every situation is different, and everybody has their own way of dealing with this, but be prepared with action plans should such a situation arise rather than being caught off guard.

5. WHAT TO DO DURING A POWER FAILURE

I have experienced power failures a few times while in a busy clinic in different locations. If there is a brief lapse in power, it does not usually have a significant impact on much, other than electronic items that need to be reset.

You should always be aware of back-up power, and what is available in your setup. If you are in a bigger building, there will likely be a generator that will kick in when there's a power failure. In the event of a generator, some limited light and elevator use will usually be possible.

The following scenarios and options relate to a power failure that lasts well beyond a few minutes. While much of this might seem like common sense to you now, when you actually experience a situation like this, it might not seem that simple.

5.1 Ground-or low-floor practice

An advantage of being on a low floor in the event of a power failure is that it will enable easier access to your office without the use of an elevator, which might be only available for emergency use, or not function at all during a power failure. Low floors will obviously be better for limit your older patients, or those with disabilities where climbing stairs is not an option.

The first consideration before looking at options is whether there is adequate lighting. If there is a large amount of natural light present, then there is potential that things can continue, obviously dependent on what type of practice you have. Patients can still be processed and examined, but some things will have to wait, such as data entry or any procedures needing extra light or equipment that require electrical outlets. This will be more of a challenge in an office that is exclusively utilizing an electronic format, as no patient files will be able to be obtained.

5.2 Higher floor office

This scenario is more challenging, as your patient visits will be significantly limited by elevator use, or lack thereof. If there is enough natural light, it is feasible that you can finish off with the visits of the patients already there, but patients booked later will likely not be able to get to you, other than walking up 15 flights of stairs for example. Depending on the need of technology for office functioning, you might not be able to finish with the patients who are already in the office. In this case, you may have to hang a sign saying you are closed until the power has been restored.

6. OUTDATED PATIENT CONTACT DETAILS

For many good reasons it is imperative to always have up-to-date information for your patients at all times, as was mentioned briefly in Chapter 12. Patients often forget to notify doctors' offices of a change in address or other contact information. This is particularly a problem when patients make infrequent visits to you office, and this important notification of change has slipped their mind. This is of major significance when you get an abnormal result for a patient and you can't get hold of him or her. I recall several situations in my office with all of us scrambling to get hold of a patient when contact details were invalid, and an abnormal test result needed some follow-up.

There are some steps that your office can take to avoid potential problems in this regard. One thing is for office staff to always ask patients when they arrive if there has been a change in address, but this can be quite cumbersome, or easily forgotten with each patient. Another way is for patients to fill out a form for every visit, but this, once again, can be a burden on the patient and your front staff. I think that whatever your office decides on, something has to be done to ensure current contact information is available when you are ordering any type of investigation. It is simply dangerous to have an abnormal result come back to you when the patient cannot be contacted in a timely fashion.

When I am with a patient and I am proceeding with further investigations, I have gotten into the habit of asking the patient if the phone number on file (which I read out loud) is the best number to contact him or her. The amount of times the patient tells me that number is not valid anymore is more than I would like, despite office staff making an effort to keep information up-to-date.

What can you do if you need to get hold of a patient with invalid contact information? Look through all patient records to see if there is another health-care provider who is involved in the care of the patient. If this is the case, make a call to these offices to see if any additional information can be obtained. If there is some hospital or laboratory documentation in the file, contact the hospital or lab too. You might want to phone the local hospital anyway to see if this patient is on file, or has ever made a visit to the facility. Do not forget about directory assistance or even the Internet.

If you absolutely cannot locate the patient at all, and the situation is crucial, consider contacting the police to help with the search. Be sure to document all these steps thoroughly and keep this tracking information in the patient's file.

One other point which should be mentioned, is about documenting patient conversations and attempting to contact patients for whatever reason. Both yourself and your staff should get in the habit of making notes about important phone calls and keeping this information in the patient files. You just never know when you might need this, particularly if you have to demonstrate to a patient how, and when, you tried to contact him or her.

7. BAD WEATHER

You can never predict what the weather is going to be like when appointments are booked way ahead of time. There can be thunderstorms, snowstorms, floods, and all kinds of things. Depending on the part of the world in which you work, give your patients a break during these unforeseen weather conditions. There can be so many factors as to why patients cannot make it to your office in bad weather. While many cities are well prepared for weather extremes and have the necessary resources and expertise to deal with the situations, others are caught off guard, or simply do not have the infrastructure to cope with such weather conditions.

I have always understood and empathized with patients who have not been able to make an appointment in unforeseen situations. My staff has thus rescheduled patients accordingly without penalty. I am aware of offices that charge patients for missed visits, but I would hope that consideration is given in this regard where the reason for a patient not showing up is beyond his or her control.

One thing to always keep in mind is to change your voice mail, alerting patients as to the status of your office in the event of extreme weather conditions. Either let them know that things are running as usual, or that the office is closed, and that updated information will be made available at a later time.

8. STAFF CONFLICTS

Staff conflicts are covered by entire books and there are professionals who specialize in conflict resolution alone! While I am no expert on this matter, I can only give you a few words of advice in this regard from personal experience. Unless you have good skills in the area of conflict resolution, think first and get advice before you rush into any type of mediation. There are also unions and other representation, which your staff might belong to, and saying something inappropriate might lead you into deeper trouble than just the problem you are trying to resolve in the first place. Also try and get as much background about the circumstances as you can before passing any judgment, or attempting to solve the situation.

These occurrences can be tricky for a new and inexperienced employer, so do your homework first on this one and do not be shy to ask for help. You might proactively encourage and support your staff to attend some courses relevant to the office practice, such as conflict resolution.

Checklist 6 will help you in troubleshooting situations. Make notes of whom to contact when an emergency arrives. Keep the checklist in an easily accessible place so you can have quick access to phone numbers. The checklist is also included on the CD.

TROUBLESHOOTING

1. A staff member phones in sick (options)

☐ Contact details for people who are familiar with your office, and may be able to come at short notice:

Name: _____ Phone number: _____

Name: _____ Phone number: _____

Name: _____ Phone number: _____

Name: _____ Phone number: _____

Name: _____ Phone number: _____

☐ What is your back-up plan to realign staff responsibilities temporarily?

_____

_____

☐ Phone numbers for temporary staffing agencies:

Name of Agency: _____ Phone number: _____

Name of Agency: _____ Phone number: _____

Name of Agency: _____ Phone number: _____

☐ Do you have to close the office if a staff member is away? If so, what is your back-up plan to call patients about cancelled appointments?

_____

_____

2. Potentially unsafe or compromising situation (options)

The following is an outline of what to do in unsafe or compromising situations. You may want to revise this list to suit your office:

☐ Call for help (security or 911) or building security if you sense immediate danger; push panic button if available.

☐ If you are with a patient, leave the room to reflect on the situation. If you return to the examination room, leave the door open or, even better, have a staff member accompany you.

☐ Call someone for advice or obtain advice from experts in the field.

☐ Try to prevent the situation from escalating.

☐ Debrief with office staff after the situation has passed.

3. Preparation for a fire alarm

☐ Always have a current copy of the standard building guidelines.

☐ Make sure staff are briefed on what to do in the event of a fire alarm.

☐ Do you know what to do if you are in the middle of a procedure? Follow guidelines as obtained from a local hospital or other relevant organization.

4. What to do during a power failure

☐ Analyze the situation to see if the safety of the patients and your office staff is compromised.

☐ If dark, evacuate the office as best you can (hopefully there is a back-up generator).

☐ If you are in the middle of a procedure, consider all options for ending what you are doing.

☐ If there is a lot of light on a lower floor, and it is not reliant on power, consider whether you can potentially finish a clinic.

☐ If lots of light, and on a higher floor, potential for completing visits of those in your office is an option, but subsequent patients will likely not be able to reach the office.

5. Outdated patient contact information

☐ Do you or your staff verify patient contact information for every visit? If not, what can you and your staff do to make sure you have the correct information in the future?

_____

_____

☐ Look for any other health-care provider in the file and contact that office for additional information.

☐ If there is a hospital or laboratory record in the file, contact the facility. Consider contacting the local facility even if there are no records associated with the patient.

☐ Directory assistance or web search.

☐ If absolutely crucial, consider contacting the police to help with the search for information.

☐ Document all attempts diligently in the file for future reference.

6. Bad weather conditions

☐ Change voice mail to inform patients of the situation.

7. Conflict resolution

☐ Do not rush with an attempt to solve the situation, unless impending danger.

☐ Reflect on the situation and consider an action plan.

☐ Do not hesitate to call someone for advice, if needed.

☐ Are there conflict resolution courses that staff can attend?

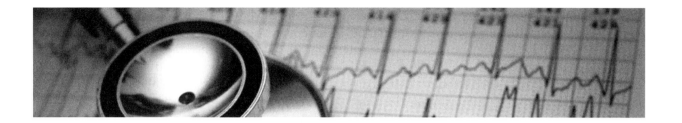

CONCLUSION

Whether you are considering a career in medicine, are about to start a brand new practice, are considering a change, or are involved in a health-care profession in some other way, being thoughtful, resourceful, and diligent are all vital to success. While this book is essentially focused on the setup of a new office for health-care professionals, I feel it would be incomplete without a more holistic approach. For me, setting up an office is part of the continuum for a career in medicine. This book is one of many sources that you can tap into when making those big and small decisions, or you are just seeking additional input along the way.

Making that right choice for going into the health-care field of your liking is, for me, the most important piece of the puzzle. Adding all the other pieces, as alluded to in this book, makes for a complete picture. There are so many different aspects to consider when you are setting up a career in medicine, or an office, that it is impossible to cover everything in one single book, or any other source for that matter. I have attempted to look hard for all those pieces, which might be quite far displaced from the final product, but all of which are needed to complete a comprehensive picture. I have concentrated on details that I would have liked to have known when I started an office for the first time, or even when I thought of a medical career at the outset.

By reading through this book, in addition to thinking about the more technical aspects of an office setup, I hope you have been able to reflect on your own specific reasons for choosing a medical career, thus making starting your practice that much more fulfilling. I trust that you have been able to pick up some ideas about how to set up and run things in your office no matter which health-care profession you are in. Having been trained by, worked with, and referred patients to so many other health-care providers, I feel there are more similarities than differences between all the health-care fields, particularly with respect to the theme of this book — start and run a medical practice. Naturally, we all, with time and experience, find our own comfort zone as to how exactly we want things to run in our offices based on our own needs and likes. The best strategy is to take bits and pieces from different sources and mold them your own unique way.

Whatever stage you are at, there is so much to learn and enjoy as you navigate your own path. I still, to this day, feel privileged and lucky to be able to contribute to the health and well-being of others. Not being wise with the different steps of the path can significantly impact on a career choice. Going into to a complex situation, such as an office setup, and being less informed will make for a more challenging experience. It is for this reason that I hope I have been able to share some wisdom from my career course to make the journey for you easier and more fulfilling.